A Further Collection of
CHINESE LYRICS

'The Poet Lin Pu Wandering in the Moonlight.'
From the hanging scroll by Tu Chin, active c. 1465–1487.
(*See p. 47*)

A Further Collection of

CHINESE LYRICS

and other Poems

Rendered into verse by
ALAN AYLING
from the translations of the Chinese by
DUNCAN MACKINTOSH
in collaboration with
CH'ENG HSI and T'UNG PING-CHENG

Calligraphy by
CHENG HSÜAN

Illustrations by
FEI CH'ENG-WU

Nashville, Tennessee
Vanderbilt University Press

Published in the United States of America 1970
by Vanderbilt University Press
Nashville, Tennessee, U.S.A.
and in Great Britain
by Routledge & Kegan Paul Ltd.
Broadway House, 68-74 Carter Lane,
London, E.C.4, England

© *Alan Ayling and Duncan Mackintosh 1969*

Library of Congress Catalog
Card Number 73-112602

ISBN 0-8265-1150-3

Printed in Great Britain

To the Memory of

NIEN

and

MEI-P'ING

CONTENTS

TZ'U

T'ANG AND FIVE DYNASTIES

SUNG DYNASTY

SOUTHERN SUNG DYNASTY

FOREWORD

by *John Smith*

(Poet, critic and Editor of *The Poetry Review*, 1962–65)

I was introduced to the enchanting world of Tz'u by the late Victor Gollancz who had been delighted by some of the work of Duncan Mackintosh and Alan Ayling and rightly suspected that I would share his pleasure. At that time I was editing *The Poetry Review* and was privileged to publish an article on this interesting Chinese verse form together with some half-dozen examples. That article became the basis of *A Collection of Chinese Lyrics* to which this present volume is the logical successor.

I must lay my cards on the table and confess at once that I am totally ignorant of the Chinese language; my knowledge of the poetry comes from translations in various styles by such poets as Ezra Pound, Witter Bynner, Harold Acton, Arthur Waley, etc., but it was not until I read the work of the present translators that I found myself so immersed in the world not only of the poetry but of the poets. It is this completeness that makes the work of Mackintosh and Ayling so fascinating. They present us with a landscape within which we may wander at our leisure, getting to know something of the background of the times, observing the temperaments and characters of the various writers, sharing something of their enjoyments and despairs. This is particularly valuable in relation to an appreciation of the poetry which is rarely abstract or in any sense metaphysical, but is rooted deeply in the private lives of the poets; even the purest of the lyrics seems to refer positively to a personal event, to a particular love. There is less distancing than in the traditional English lyric where often even the most powerful emotions are firmly confined within the realm of the art.

Translation from one European language into another is a formidable task. How much more formidable to try to render in

English poetry written in a language utterly alien from our own, following laws both of sound and structure which have no single point of contact with our own linguistic complexities and felicities. A choice has to be made at once: to be free, to attempt to catch something of the essence behind the original poem, to create a personal version, rather than to attempt a 'translation', or to pay exact respect to the original and bring across a version as close as possible to the primal meaning and structure. Where the short lyric is concerned the difficulties are truly immense.

Reference to the notes on the poems will show how these present translators have pursued their aims of trying to reflect as far as they thought reasonably possible the rhyme schemes and line lengths of the originals. The task was certainly worth tackling —even in those areas where a measure of defeat was inevitable, and acknowledged, or was accepted as a welcome avoidance of what would otherwise have been padding. For one thing this volume, together with its companion, destroys the comfortable myth that Chinese poetry was written in a sort of Lawrentian free verse, was of a permanently dying cadence and enervatingly nostalgic. Ayling and Mackintosh show us a very different facet of the lyric style, highly artificial, always rhymed and bearing not a little resemblance to our own Elizabethan poetry. The poets, too, seem not unlike our own Raleigh, Sydney, Wyatt or Campion.

The scenes have been set by Duncan Mackintosh. What a wealth of fascinating information his own experiences in China and researches have uncovered and with what delicacy, good humour and charm has he drawn for us the portraits of his chosen poets. He has rescued them from the false world of our previous conceptions. We see them not as strange beings from a world more alien than Venus or Mars, but human beings little removed from ourselves, exhibiting similar qualities of love, anger, passion, ribaldry, wit; going about their daily affairs, dealing with problems that are permanent in human nature. From this we see that the book is to be read as an entity and not merely as an annotated collection of translations. For this reason there are included certain poems which are not, in themselves particularly original or inspired but which are indicative of the personality of the poet concerned, or demonstrate some

x

aspects of the contemporaneous society. In so far as it is possible these two men, 'amateurs' in the very best sense of that sadly misused word, have given us access to the world of Tz'u.

Nowadays where the arts are concerned, we live in a savage jungle of critical in-fighting. To produce masterpieces is the demand; to show evidence of a high seriousness. But pleasure is not to be gainsaid and pleasure is what is to be obtained from a gentle perusal of this *Further Collection of Chinese Lyrics*. My own pleasure in the work is multiplied by the very real privilege it is to contribute this brief Foreword.

PREFACE

We published *A Collection of Chinese Lyrics* three years ago because the lyric form (tz'u), so popular for over 1,200 years and up to the present day with the Chinese themselves, had been somewhat neglected in English translation. As far as the lyrics are concerned, the new book covers the same field as the first but with two differences of emphasis, the first of which is to be found in the poets to whom we have given the most prominence, and the second in the inclusion of some early Chinese (twelfth century) music with the lyrics for which it was composed. (See Acknowledgements, p. xx.)

In our earlier book we gave pride of place to the poet and tragic sovereign Li Yü (A.D. 937–978), supreme master of the poignant lyric, of whose tz'u we offered nineteen. This time we have turned instead to two robust civil servants whose vigorous minds, fresh outlook and keen observation introduced a new dimension to a form that had relied traditionally on the pangs of parting and separation and hopeless longing. About a third of the lyrics in our new book is the work of Su Shih (better known as Su Tung-p'o) (A.D. 1036–1101), and of Hsin Ch'i-chi (A.D. 1140–1207).

Su Shih, of whose work we printed a few particularly well-known lyrics in our first volume, rescued the tz'u from being a vehicle for expressing what one modern Chinese writer has called 'sentimental drivel', and injected into it his searching, ebullient, forthright and humorous spirit. His was the more difficult task because he had to break away from a tradition in suitable subject matter which had been firmly laid down over the previous century. Hsin Ch'i-chi, who wrote exclusively in this verse-form and who was represented by only four lyrics in our earlier volume, while carrying on Su Shih's disregard for the 'propriety' of this old tradition, had the sharpening experience in his lifetime of seeing half the empire, and his own home, lost to the invading Chin Tartars. Parenthetically it is interesting

xiii

to read in Professor Yoshikawa's *An Introduction to Sung Poetry* (translated by Burton Watson and published by Harvard University Press, 1967), that while he expresses the view that the tz'u 'as a rule, was used almost exclusively to express minor states of emotion' he specifically mentions that 'there are exceptions in the works of Su Tung-p'o and Hsin Ch'i-chi'.

The second difference in emphasis lies in the inclusion, with Chiang K'uei's (A.D. 1155–1229) own lyrics, of the tunes to which they were written to be sung; of these five tunes at least three were composed by this poet-musician himself. His music, hitherto undeciphered, has been transcribed into staff-notation in the course of only the last twenty years or so. It is particularly due to Dr Laurence Picken's research and deep knowledge of oriental music, including the music of Central Asia which had such an important bearing on the tunes associated with the Chinese tz'u in the T'ang Dynasty, that we are able not only to recapture its original appeal but to perceive the regularity of rhythm lying behind an irregularity of verse-pattern, that is, of length of line. (This point is dealt with in greater detail in 'Note on the Tz'u', p. xv). It is interesting to recall that at roughly this same period (thirteenth century) secular poet-musicians in France were writing lyrics to their own compositions in a recognized custom of that time which has not often been repeated since. These troubadours and trouvères wrote both their lyrics and tunes to a regular verse-form and rhythmical pattern.

It will be noticed that the most recent tz'u in this collection was written by Ch'eng Hsi, whose help and encouragement during the preparation of this volume and its predecessor has been so much appreciated. We include it not only on its merits as a lyric – it describes in terms of a typhoon the impact of the Japanese invasion and occupation of parts of China in the third decade of this century, a period sometimes overlooked in the light of more recent events – but also because it illustrates how the tz'u is still being employed by poets to express their emotions. The fact that Mao Tse-tung has been expressing himself in this lyric form over the last forty years or so is too well known for comment.

Although this collection is primarily of lyrics – sixty of them – we have also included two long narrative poems by the great

xiv

T'ang poet, Po Chü-i. Both these are famous pieces in the regulated verse of seven characters to each line, and both have been translated into English several times, notably by H. A. Giles in prose (*A Short History of Chinese Literature*, published by D. Appleton, 1901), Witter Bynner (*The Jade Mountain*, published by Alfred Knopf, 1931), Soame Jenyns (*The Poems of the T'ang Dynasty – A Further Selection*, published by John Murray, 1944) and F. T. Cheng. Only the last-named, in his book *East and West* (published by Hutchinson in 1951) used the Chinese rhyming pattern. As a Chinese, he felt rhymes to be as essential an ornamentation in these two long poems as in the originals. So it is that, as with the lyrics, we have followed F. T. Cheng in using rhyme, albeit somewhat loosely at times, as an ornamentation in these two poems, and in the pattern of the original. We have also translated and rendered them into verse line for line, preserving seven beats a line throughout to echo the seven characters in a line of the 'shih'.

There are glorious passages in each of these narrative poems; but some readers may find their development disconcerting, and may imagine how differently the material would have been handled by a European poet, more particularly by one of the Romantics.

Finally, in this collection we offer less poignancy and heart-break, more observation of mankind and his surroundings; of country festivals and farming, of astronomy and surf-riding, of fossils and big-game hunting, of wars and hostile frontiers, of birds and fishing. But there will of course be found among the lyrics offered the ever-recurring nostalgia and sense of loss, traditionally so much a part of the Chinese lyrical inspiration.

D. R. M.
A. F. G. A.

CHIANG K'UEI

P'u-Yü Mei Ling
(*To the tune-title 'Jade Plum Blossom, a short Lyric'*)

Su   su hsüeh p'ien.   San ju hsi-nan yüan.   Ch'un han so chiu chia t'ing kuan.

Yu yü mei chi   shu.   Pei li   yüan tung fêng.   Kao hua wei t'u.   An hsiang i   yüan.

Kung lai ling lüeh.   Mei hua nêng ch'üan.   Hua chang hao,   yüan Kung kêng chien.

Pien jou ch'un   wei chiu.   Chien hsüeh tso hsin shih.   P'an i jih,   jao hua ch'ien chuan.

For verse see Poem 53, p. 171.

NOTE ON THE TZ'U: LINE-LENGTH AND RHYTHM

A brief reference to Chiang K'uei's music was made in the Preface to this book. Little of the T'ang and Sung music has come down to us and Chiang K'uei's tunes lay undeciphered for centuries. However, in the last twenty years or so they have been transcribed into staff-notation by several Chinese scholars. Laurence Picken has gone further to show that though the lines of the lyrics consisted of an irregular number of Chinese characters, the tunes were almost certainly 'four-square'; that is, the musical lines were composed to a rhythmic measure of eight beats. In the light of his work on these tunes, it is worth expanding on these two seemingly conflicting characteristics of the tz'u – its irregularity of line-length and regularity of musical rhythm.

It must be remembered that the tz'u was developed from the shih, a verse-form of completely regular pattern, with either five or seven characters to a line running throughout the poem and with strict rules of rhyme and tonal sequence. The first departures from this pattern were known as Ch'ang-tuan Chü ('Long and short lines') and Shih-yü ('Remnants of the Shih'); the last name, indeed, as Professor Yoshikawa has pointed out (in *An Introduction to Sung Poetry* – translated by Burton Watson, Harvard University Press, 1967) suggests that it was 'an offshoot of the shih form'.

The introduction of foreign music in the T'ang Dynasty (A.D. 618–907) from Central Asia and elsewhere from the west, was one of the important factors in this development, and the name tz'u (lyric) came to be firmly applied to the new form. The foreign tunes were popular but needed Chinese words. Gradually, under the influence of such enthusiasts as Wen T'ing-yün (about A.D. 820–870), lyrics (tz'u) were specially written for these new tunes for a popular and wide-spread clientele. The song-tunes of that time were sung (for the most part) one-note-to-one syllable. When a tune made use of notes of more than one time-value (i.e. if there were the equivalents of our quavers, crochets and minims) this usually resulted in an irregular number of notes, and therefore of syllables (Chinese characters), in the lines of verse. It was this marked irregularity of line-length which most obviously distinguished tz'u from shih. Regularity of rhythm combined with irregularity of line-length can at once be recognized in our own lyrics if we look at a music-hall tune like

> Daisy, Daisy,
> Give me your answer, do.
> . . . .
> But you'd look sweet upon the seat
> Of a bicycle made for two.

These 'irregular' lines, consisting of four, six, . . . eight, eight syllables respectively, all have the same musical length of four beats. In the different lines, syllables are sung to notes of different lengths: few syllables require longer notes; many syllables, shorter notes.

In these earlier stages, even 200 years after Wen T'ing-yün, poets like Liu Yung (about A.D. 1045) and Chou Pang-yen (A.D. 1057–1121), wrote their tz'u to existing tunes and tune-patterns, specifically to be sung; the tz'u in fact was closely associated with its music. Chiang K'uei, early in the thirteenth century, himself a musician, composed new tunes for his lyrics and, stimulated as we know by his patron Fan Ch'êng-ta, sought out some of the older tunes. It could well be said then that the music, with its regular beat, 'masked' an irregularity in line-length and gave scope for rhythmic variety within the strict framework of the eight-beat measure.

But as time passed after the initial influx of music bearing well-known names ('The Fisherman', 'The Water-clock' and so on) old tunes must have been lost or forgotten, or were simply not available to a poet. Su Shih, for example, is likely to have written many of his tz'u to the tune-*pattern*, calling for so many characters to each line, without having the tune itself at his disposal, and the same could almost certainly be said of Hsin Ch'i-chi and Lu Yu, both of whom turned out great numbers of tz'u. Even if the music to the tune-patterns they adopted had still been kept alive in the capital cities, these two poets exemplified the government official serving in far outposts where no such aids to memory would be available. We see then the *pattern*, the number of notes to the musical line, stripped of its musical clothing and standing out as the most marked characteristic of the tz'u: the irregularity of line-length in the verse. (There were other characteristics, such as much more difficult patterns of rhyme and tonal sequence than were laid down for the shih, but these were matters of degree rather than of fundamental verse-form.) By the eighteenth century books of reference on the tz'u such as the Ch'in Ting Tz'u P'u, compiled to the order of the Emperor K'ang Hsi, and the Tz'u Lü produced by Wan Shu (which formed our main source for the compilation of Appendix II) set out the patterns of hundreds of tunes, without a note of music.

For the last 700 years or so, the tz'u has virtually been separated from its music, but writers today, such as Ch'eng Hsi, translated in this volume, follow in the footsteps of Su Shih and Hsin Ch'i-chi, using some of the same patterns to which the sovereign poet Li Yü wrote his tz'u a thousand years ago. The name 'tz'u' in fact has long been synonymous with 'irregularity' and no doubt this freedom in at least one dimension – line-length – found a responsive stimulus in poets exploring new fields of metre and pattern in the world of words, after the centuries of 'regularity' in the shih. It is the more fascinating that, thanks to modern scholarship, we have had uncovered for us a link between the tz'u of post-Sung days – surrounded by a slight aura of the chess-board, with its formal lay-out and intricate manœuvre – and its tuneful antecedents of a past millennium.

TRANSLATOR'S NOTE

Most of the Chinese calligraphy has been written, at our request, to include punctuation marks. We hope the purist will forgive this small divergence from the traditional writing of tz'u without punctuation. Modern Chinese editions almost invariably do now use such marks and it undoubtedly helps the reader of Chinese who is not conversant with the irregularity of line and pattern.

We have taken the advice of one reviewer who suggested we should include at least one piece of contemporary (Sung) Chinese writing. The lyric represented on page 246 is Yüeh Fei's famous tz'u (translated in our first collection and reprinted here for convenience sake in 'Notes on Poems', p. 247) reproduced from a stone-engraving of what purports to be Yüeh Fei's own calligraphy.

We ask for licence for having used the word 'guitar' as a translation of the Chinese 'p'i p'a' in the first of the two long poems (p. 205). The p'i p'a was in fact a lute, but this word now carries in English such medieval, biblical and languishing overtones that we preferred the more vibrant 'guitar' as have other translators.

We have, as before, included an Appendix I of 'Notes on the Poems'. For readers not conversant with Chinese these notes provide references to earlier classics and to literary allusions without which some parts of the poems might be incomprehensible. On page 244 of this Appendix we set out an example of an actual working translation – character by character – of one poem. This illustrates more clearly than can otherwise be explained to those unfamiliar with the language how – to quote from our first volume – 'the absence in general from Chinese poetry of verbal inflection, genders and pronouns, prepositions and conjunctions, and its epigrammatic and allusive qualities, provide their own humbling difficulties, both in translation and in subsequent versification'.

We have also included for easy reference an Appendix II (p. 263) setting out the tune-patterns. These give for each tune-title (p'u), noted at the head of each poem, the numbers of characters in each line of the Chinese texts. It will be seen that line-length in the case of the lyric (tz'u) is almost always irregular, and this irregularity has been generally reflected in the English translations. Our 'Note on the Tz'u – Line-length and Rhythm' on page xv goes into more detail and explains how this irregularity developed and how it was consonant with regularity of rhythm in the original tunes.

We have also accepted advice to include an English version of the tune-titles (p'u) for all but one or two where we have been unable to arrive at a satisfactory solution. Very few indeed of the tune-titles have any connection at all with the meaning of the verse – Chang Chih-ho's poem (No. 2, p. 9) is an exception and the tune is appropriately called 'The Fisherman' – and there is inevitably some risk of the reader being distracted; for instance the tune-title of the first poem (Wei Ying-wu's, No. 1, p. 5) is 'A Song of Laughter' whereas the verse itself deals with hopeless separation. In a few cases, therefore, we have added an appropriate title for the verse below the tune-title.

Kindly critics have also emphasized our problems about whether to provide transliterations (not always felicitous) of such words as names of places or people, or alternatively translations of such words (not always felicitous either). Recognizing this difficulty we have tried to steer a middle course – a not un-typical example of these difficulties arose in the first poem (line 3, p. 5) and the problem over the place-name Yen-chih-shan is covered in 'Notes on Poems', p. 235.

D. R. M.

ACKNOWLEDGEMENTS

The ability to translate verse of this nature without assistance from Chinese sources is given to few and I certainly could not have approached the task had it not been for the guidance of Ch'eng Hsi with his wide knowledge of his country's poetry, and for the scholarly help of T'ung Ping-cheng. It is with the greatest appreciation therefore that their names are included on the title-page, though for any mistakes, or misinterpretations of their advice in the very few instances I have gone against that advice, the responsibility will be mine not theirs.

We are grateful to Cheng Hsüan of Hong Kong for his excellent calligraphy. Ch'eng Hsi has kindly written out for us the Chinese for his own tz'u (p. 200).

Fei Ch'eng-wu has once again given us illustrations to embellish the book and bring out the background for five poems. We acknowledge with thanks permission by the Cleveland Museum of Art, John L. Severance Fund, to reproduce the painting of 'The Poet Lin Pu Wandering in the Moonlight' as a frontispiece, and Mr Ronald Somervell's kindness in allowing us to reproduce a rubbing from a memorial tablet to the poet Su Shih.

Dr Laurence Picken's work on Chiang K'uei's music – of which we print five examples – is dealt with at greater length in the Preface, in the Note on the Tz'u (p. xv), and in the biographical note on Chiang K'uei (p. 163). For the permission to reprint these pieces, which add so much to this collection, we are most grateful both to him personally and to the Editorial Board of the Hungarian Studia Musicologica (where they first appeared in the Studia's *Tomus 8*, pp. 125–172, 1966).

As author and critic, one of a small band of consistently creative writers of living lyric poetry, and a former editor of the *Poetry Review*, John Smith delighted us when he agreed to provide a Foreword to this volume. We owe him a special debt once more for the skill and generosity he has shown in providing so much constructive help and criticism.   D. R. M.

TZ'U

T'ang and Five Dynasties

WEI YING WU

(about A.D. 735–790)

Wei Ying-wu came from north of the T'ang Dynasty capital of Ch'ang-an and rose to be a Governor of Soochow. He was a man of few desires, generous temperament, and fastidious habit. He was said not to sit down to a meal until the room had been thoroughly swept and scented with burnt incense. The great poet Su Shih highly admired his poetry.

調笑　　　　　　　　　韋應物

胡馬、胡馬、遠放燕支山下。跑沙跑雪獨嘶。東望西望
路迷。迷路、迷路、邊草無窮日暮。

河漢、河漢、曉挂秋城漫漫。愁人起望相思。江南塞北
別離。離別、離別、河漢雖同路絕。

1

P'u – Tiao Hsiao

ON THE FRONTIER

Tartar horses,
Tartar horses,
Ranging wild and far at the foot of Yen-chih-shan.
One has galloped through sand and snow and now with a
neigh
Looks to the east, looks to the west, has lost its way;
Its way is lost,
Its way is lost
On the endless plains of the border as evening follows day.

Milky Way,
Milky Way
Above the city wall at autumn dawn hung wide.
A restless watcher yearns and gazes sick at heart;
The river south, the border north, so far apart;
Apart so far,
Apart so far;
For us, the Milky Way; all other roads are cut.

CHANG CHIH HO

(about A.D. 730–810)

As a boy Chang Chih-ho showed great promise, and by the age of sixteen was passing classical examinations. He entered government service and was employed in the Han-lin Academy, proof alone of outstanding literary ability. He lost his post for a period, but when the offer of reinstatement came he refused to return and instead retired to a life on the water, living and moving about in boats. This was his abiding interest; he enjoyed fishing – he called himself 'The Fisherman in the Mist' – but was said to do so, at any rate in later life, without using bait. Here he followed in the footsteps of Chiang Tzu-ya, one of the early creators of the Chou Dynasty (1122–255 B.C.), who 'fished with a straight hook'.

Su Shih greatly admired the poem on 'The Fisherman' selected here, but on the grounds that he could not find the original tune, set himself to add a few words so that it would fit the tune Wan Ch'i Sha ('Washing Silk by the Stream'). The result is not an improvement and only opens him to the Chinese saying about those who embellish unnecessarily – that he 'drew a snake and then added feet to it' (hua shê t'ien tsu)!

Chang Chih-ho was a man of wide interests and an excellent landscape painter. Fortified by wine he used to play on flute and drum. As was so often the case in the literary appraisals of these times, speed of composition was commented on as a feature of exceptional ability. Li Po and Wen T'ing-yün for instance were said to dash off their verse. With Chang Chih-ho it was his speed in painting that was specially mentioned.

漁父　　　　　　張志和

西塞山前白鷺飛。桃花流水鱖魚肥。青箬笠、綠簑衣。
斜風細雨不須歸。

釣臺漁父褐爲裘。兩兩三三艇艋舟。能縱棹、慣乘流。
長江白浪不曾憂。

2

P'u – Yü Fu
(*To the tune-title 'The Fisherman'*)

I

In front of Hsi-sai-shan the herons fly in white
Where peach trees blossom and water flows and mandarin
fish grow fat.
With his rain-hat bamboo-green
And his cape the green of grass
What need to turn about though wind and drizzle drive
across?

II

With coarsest cloth for furs the fisher takes his stand
By other little boats in twos and threes around.
So skilful with his oar
And trained to ride the stream
The countless waves of the Great River have never troubled
him.

雲溪灣裏釣魚翁。艋艋為家西復東。江上雪、浦邊風。笑著荷衣不歎窮。

松江蟹舍主人歡。菰飯蓴羹亦共餐。楓葉落、荻花乾。醉宿漁舟不覺寒。

III

There's an old fisherman living in Cha-hsi bay;
His home's his boat as east or west he makes his way.
When snow is on the river
And wind across the strait
He doesn't whine because he's poor but smiles in his thin
coat.

IV

The crabber, happy host, in his hut by the Sung river
Has mushrooms, rice, and cress for soup; they feast
together.
Though maple leaves are fallen
And reed plumes dry and old,
In a drunken sleep on his fishing boat he doesn't feel the
cold.

漁父

青艸湖中
月正圓
巴陵漁父
棹歌連
釣車子
概頭船
樂在風波
不用仙

張志和

V

On the Ch'ing-ts'ao Lake, just at the full of the moon,
  Pa-ling fishermen row, taking turns with a tune;
      Then armed with fishing reels,
      Their boats staked at the bow,
Happy in wind and wave they wouldn't exchange with
      immortals now.

PO CHÜ I

(A.D. 772–846)

Po Chü-i's personal experience of the ups and downs of an official's life – promotion and prosperity when in favour, and dismissal and temporary banishment when out of favour – led him to deal with this subject in his verse; it is for instance well brought out in his long poem' The Song of a Guitar' (p. 205). Nature's rhythmic cycles, of spring and autumn and of sun and moon, were regularly repeated as opposed to the evanescence of man's life. In the lyric selected here Po Chü-i chose to draw his comparisons on what we should today call a geological scale. He was almost certainly quoting from a T'ang Dynasty writer who based himself on sources written some hundreds of years earlier. (For further details see Appendix I, Notes on Poems, Stanza V, line 2, p. 236). Po Chü-i writing in the ninth century – incidentally some 600 years before the Renaissance – must have read this material and found it a striking illustration with which to point his thoughts on the vicissitudes of man's life.

浪淘沙　　　　白居易

一泊沙來一泊去。一重浪滅一重生。
相攪相淘無歇日、會教山海一時平。

白浪茫茫與海連。平沙浩浩四無邊。
朝去暮來淘不住、遂令東海變桑田。

3

P'u – Lang T'ao Sha
(To the tune-title 'The Waves Scouring the Sand')

I

One wave brings the sand, another sucks it back again;
One wave dies away, another wave is born.
This constant stirring and scouring of wave on sand
Turns at last the hills and seas to level land.

II

White waves everywhere are melted into ocean;
Unendingly the level sands spread wider all around.
Morning passes, evening falls, the scouring does not end;
Finally the mighty seas are turned to farming land.

青草湖中萬里程。黃梅雨裏一人行。

愁見灘頭夜泊處、風翻暗浪打船聲。

借問江潮與海水。何似君情與妾心。

相恨不如潮有信、相思始覺海非深。

III

To the Ch'ing-ts'ao lake is an interminable journey;
Travel alone in apricot time with the rain pouring
And the dismal sight of a bank of sand for the night's mooring
And the wind tossing the dark waves to slap on the boat.

IV

Ask the waters of the tides and the ocean
What a man's affections or a girl's heart are like.
Lovers' feelings are not changeless like the tidal flow
And ocean's depths to those who share true love appear shallow.

海底飛塵終有日。山頭化石豈無時。

誰道小郎拋小婦、船頭一去沒回期。

隨波逐浪到天涯。遷客生還有幾家。

却到帝鄉重富貴、請君莫忘浪淘沙。

V

The dust will have its day and fly where ocean had its bed:
A time will come when fossils lie exposed among the hills.
And who can swear a callow boy has cast his wife away?
Can a ship that's outward bound not return one day?

VI

Swept afar by each successive wave to the horizon,
Of all who suffered banishment, how many have survived?
But should Imperial favour make you once more rich and grand
Please, Sir, never forget the waves scouring the sand!

WEI CHUANG

(about A.D. 855–920)

Wei Chuang was a native of Tu-ling in the province of Shensi.
The family was very poor but the young boy extremely diligent.
He went up to the capital, Ch'ang-an, for his literary examina-
tion and while there – when he was only twenty-five years old –
was caught up in the Huang-ch'ao rebellion against the T'ang
Dynasty and fled with his family to Chiang-nan province, south
of the Yangtze River. It is of the years he spent there that he
writes so warmly in his lyrics, swearing that he will never go
back north to his native province until forced, by strong tradi-
tion, to retire and be buried there.

Later in life, by which time the revolt had been put down, he
passed his 'chin-shih' doctorate (A.D. 894) and served at the
Court of the T'ang Emperor Chao Tsung. Later still (A.D. 901)
he was invited to assist in the administration of one of the
principalities, of Shu (now known as Szechuan), and when the
T'ang Dynasty collapsed and Shu established itself as an
independent kingdom he became its Prime Minister.

The straitened circumstances of his early life are said to
have made him very mean, and he must have been a terror to his
household. Food and fuel had to be carefully weighed and it was
even said that the rice had to be counted grain by grain.

In the first stanza of the following lyric he describes his
memories of his early love in the North; in the second stanza,
his feelings as a young exile making his way among the metro-
politan pleasures of the South, and how these pleasures still
grip him; in the last stanza he reverts, on a note of remorse,
to his youth in Loyang.

菩薩蠻　　　　韋　莊

紅樓別夜堪惆悵。香燈半卷流蘇帳。殘月出門時。美
人和淚辭。琵琶金翠羽。絃上黃鶯語。勸我早還家。綠
窗人似花。

4

P'u – P'u Sa Man
(*To the tune-title 'The Strange Goddesses'*)

NORTH AND SOUTH

I

Parting at night in the upper room what preys to grief we
were –
Lamp-lit fragrance and those half-rolled tasselled curtains
there.
The moon was waning as I left the house;
Your beauty shone in every farewell tear.

Your gilt guitar, king-fisher blue inlaid,
Its strings a golden-oriole's serenade,
Urged me to come back soon, to come back soon
To the green-gauze window veiling a flower-fresh maid.

如今却憶江南樂。當時年少春衫薄。騎馬倚斜橋。滿樓紅袖招。翠屏金屈曲。醉入花叢最宿。此度見花枝。白頭誓不歸。

洛陽城裏春光好。洛陽才子他鄉老。柳暗魏王堤。此時心轉迷。桃花春水淥。水上鴛鴦浴。凝恨對殘暉。憶君君不知。

II

Those happy days at Chiang-nan, what memories now they
bring!
Then I was a youngster, wore a flimsy shirt in spring
And rested my horse on top of a hump-backed bridge
By houses full of red sleeves beckoning.

That kingfisher-coloured screen with hinges of gold!
I drank and revelled in haunts of love night-long.
And this time, now I've seen such beauty in flower
I swear I won't go back until I am old.

III

Loyang! Inside those city walls the springs are shining fair
But the scholars born in Loyang have been growing old
elsewhere.
Duke Wei's canal was veiled in shady willow
The day my heart was taken prisoner!

Peach-blossom buds by green spring waters blow;
Mandarin ducks bathe in the river's flow.
Plunged in regret I face the setting sun,
Thinking of you; but this you do not know.

菩薩蠻　　　　　無名氏

牡丹含露真珠顆，美人折向庭前過；含笑問檀郎：花強妾貌強？檀郎故相惱，須道花枝好。一面發嬌嗔，碎挼花打人。

ANON. (WU MING SHIH)

5

P'u – P'u Sa Man
(*To the tune-title 'The Strange Goddesses'*)

Peonies cradle the dew; every drop a pearl.
Turning off the path beside the house a pretty girl
Smiles and calls up to her boy
'Is this flower the prettier or am I?'
When, just to tease her, he
Says, 'Of course, the peony',
A show of pique, a sudden whim,
She flings the crumpled bloom at him!

FÊNG YEN SSU

(about A.D. 903–960)

Fêng Yen-ssu (who is also known as Fêng Yen-chi) rose to be Prime Minister to the second ruler Li Ying (Ching) of the Southern T'ang Dynasty. His lyrics are highly rated by critics and in particular by the nineteenth-century writer Wang Kuo-wei; many rank them second only to those of Li Yü, the third and last ruler of the Southern T'ang, who is generally acknowledged to be the greatest writer of tz'u. Fêng Yen-ssu has been described as a highly intelligent, cold and ambitious person but he mellowed later in life and his tz'u are warm and sensitive.

In one of the verses selected here (Poem No. 8) he sets his scene – one of ageless application – at the time of the spring festival of Ch'ing-ming (Pure Brightness) when the jilted girl could be sure that her young man would at least come back to his home town. For it was at this festival that each family gathered at the graves of their ancestors to pay their respects. The eve of the festival was called Han-shih (literally 'Cold Food') for traditionally no fuel was to be burnt (the poet specifically refers to 'Han-shih' in line 4 of the Chinese, translated here as 'at Ch'ing-ming Eve').

This custom of no cooking arose from a legend about one Chieh Chih-t'ui, who went into exile with a Prince of Ch'in in the seventh century B.C. On the Prince's return to power some years later Chieh refused all offers of reward or position and disappeared with his mother into the woods. The Prince was determined to find his faithful friend and having failed up till then finally decided to smoke him out by setting the forest on fire. But Chieh and his mother would not move and were later found burnt to death. The Prince was so upset that it was decreed that no fuel should be burnt in the third month of the year, all food being eaten cold. This law was abolished in a later reign but Ennin, the Japanese Buddhist Priest who visited China in the ninth century A.D. notes that cold food was eaten for a period of three days at the time of the spring festival.

謁金門　　　馮延巳

風乍起。吹縐一池春水。閑引鴛鴦香徑裏。手挼紅杏蕊。

鬥鴨欄干獨倚。碧玉搔頭斜墜。終日望君君不至。舉頭聞鵲喜。

6

P'u – Yeh Chin Mên
(*To the tune-title 'Visit to the Golden Gate'*)

A wind suddenly rises
And blows into wrinkles the face of the spring-water pond.
Idling by on the flowery pathway she calls to the mandarin
ducks,
Crumpling a rose-pink apricot bloom in her hand.

Absorbed by a frieze of battling drakes she leans on the
balustrade,
Her green jade hairpin falling awry.
'I have watched for you all day long, but you do not come'
– and then
She lifts her head, hearing the magpie!

醉花間　　　　　　馮延巳

晴雪小園春未到。池邊梅自早。高樹鵲銜巢，斜月明寒草。山川風景好。自古金陵道。少年看却老。相逢莫厭醉金杯，別離多、懽會少。

7

Clear skies, and snow in the little garden; though spring's
not come
There, by the pond, is an early blossoming plum.
Magpies build their nests in the tall trees:
Waning moonlight gleams on the cold grass.

Mountain and river: how beautiful the scene
By the Chin-ling road, just as it's always been.
But youth will age so soon in me, in you,
That when we meet you mustn't refuse to empty the
golden cup;
For life's good-byes are many,
Its joyful meetings, few.

鵲踏枝　　　　　馮延巳

幾日行雲何處去。忘卻歸來、不道春將暮。百草千花寒食路。香車繫在誰家樹。

淚眼倚樓頻獨語。雙燕飛來、陌上相逢否。撩亂春愁如柳絮。悠悠夢裏無尋處。

8

P'u – Ch'iao T'a Chih
(*To the tune-title 'Magpies on a Branch'*)

'So long away, my cloud; where did he disappear?
Has he forgotten to return?
Doesn't he know the end of spring is near?
With trees a mass of blossom by the road at Ch'ing-ming
Eve
His carriage must have halted – at whose door?'

Leaning from her lonely room she murmurs tearfully
'You pair of swallows, in your flight
Above the road-side, did you pass him by?'
And so with longings whirled away like willow-down in
spring
She wanders on in dreams unendingly.

Sung Dynasty

P'AN LANG

(about A.D. 950)

P'an Lang writes in the poem translated here of Hangchow which lies between the sea to the east, the Ch'ien-tang River on its south side and the West Lake and its hills to the west – a site of great natural beauty. Two hundred years after P'an Lang wrote this it was to become the capital of the Southern Sung Dynasty, and 150 years later still Marco Polo visited it.

P'an Lang in his second stanza describes the Ch'ien-tang River bore, which for hundreds of years has drawn great crowds at the time of the autumn spring tides. Dr Fitch in *Hangchow Itineraries* in 1929 wrote of the first advancing wave reaching a vertical height of 22 feet and added that 'the roar of the approaching tide can be heard for 45 minutes before it passes the beholder. The white crest, ever changing, can be seen for a half-hour before its arrival. . . .'

The sport of coming in on the crest of the bore dates back probably well before P'an Lang, but about a hundred years later (in about A.D. 1065) a local governor issued an order forbidding it as being too dangerous. Two hundred years later, however, a writer adds that 'it has not been possible to stop it'.

It is difficult to tell from the Chinese how these 'surf-riders' came in, whether in small craft, on boards, or floating on the crest, holding their scarlet banners above their heads. The sport was certainly a highly dangerous one for many lives were lost every year.

Needless to say the appearance of this giant wave was associated with a supernatural cause and to venture out in order to ride in on the bore's crest was known as going out 'to meet Wu Tzu-hsü'. The legend concerns a general and great states-man, Wu Tzu–hsü, of the Wu Kingdom whose southern boundary was the Ch'ien-tang River. Wu Tzu–hsü begged his ruler to beware of the intentions of his southern neighbour, the

41

Kingdom of Yüeh. However, his advice was rejected and he was furthermore forced to commit suicide. He took the precaution of telling his son to wrap up his body in a fish's skin and throw it into the river, for he would then be able to move up and down with the tide and witness the invasion he had foretold – and which indeed came about.

酒泉子　　　潘　閬

長憶西湖，畫日憑闌樓上望。三三兩兩釣魚舟，島嶼

正清秋。笛聲依約蘆花裏，白鳥成行忽驚起。別來閒

整釣魚竿，思入水雲寒。

長憶觀潮，滿郭人爭江上望。來疑滄海盡成空，萬面

鼓聲中。弄潮兒向濤頭立，手把紅旗旗不溼。別來幾

向夢中看，夢覺尚心寒

9

P'u – Chiu Ch'üan Tzu
(To the tune-title 'The Spring of Wine')

I

I often remember the Western Lake;
I used to look out on it all day long
        as I leant on the upper railing.
Fishing boats in twos and threes were there
And little islands, just as early autumn light shone clear.

Flute notes quavered somewhere among the reeds,
        remote and thin;
And white birds suddenly startled rose
        together and formed in line.
Since I left whenever I've time
        to look over my fishing rod
My thoughts go back to the lake, misty and cold.

II

I often remember watching the tidal bore;
Riverside crowds from all around the district
        jostled to see.
As it came, I imagined the mighty ocean
        would empty itself on me,
Thronged with the clamour of tens of thousands of drums.

The tidal-riders poised upright
        on the lip of the giant wave.
Scarlet banners in their hands
        and never a banner wet.
Since I left, how often the sight
        returns in my dreams
And I wake with the cold thrill of it on me yet.

LIN PU

(A.D. 967–1028)

Lin Pu, like P'an Lang before him, is one of the few poets of any stature who never took government office. He spent his whole life at Hangchow living alone on Solitary Hill overlooking the West Lake, where his tomb lies today. There he wrote poetry, cultivated plum trees and kept cranes as companions. For twenty years he was said never even to have gone into the city, less than a mile away, and as a result to have 'plum blossom as a wife and cranes as sons'. If a visitor came to see him while he was out on the lake his servant would let out the cranes to call him back; the evidence for this story probably arises from the name of a little kiosk on the hill, 'The Pavilion of the Release of the Cranes'.

In case this gives too exaggerated an idea of a recluse's life it must be added that Lin Pu had a great number of girl friends.

He was chiefly known for his 'regular' poetry (shih) and few of his lyrics (tz'u) have come down to us. The reference to the Wu and Yüeh hills in the tz'u chosen for this collection is a reminder of the division made by the Ch'ien-t'ang River between the two Kingdoms, of Wu on the north and Yüeh on the south. Furthermore the last line – 'Already the tide runs deep in the estuary' – deals (as does P'an Lang's tz'u, see p. 45) with the arrival of that river's tidal bore. Whereas P'an Lang writes of the autumn bore of great height, there was of course a twice-daily incoming tidal wave only a foot or two high which brought, even in this translator's days, enough water over the bar to let the junks in and out of the city's anchorage. A peaceful collection of idle junks would suddenly be galvanized by the arrival of the bore into a fluster of activity, and with much banging of gongs and rattling of oars on the decks, the fleet would set off into the open sea.

A reproduction of a painting of the poet Lin Pu forms the frontispiece.

長相思　　　　　林逋

吳山青，越山青，兩岸青山相送迎，誰知離別情？君淚盈，妾淚盈，羅帶同心結未成，江頭潮已平。

10

Wu hill growing green,
Yüeh hill growing green,
Two green hill river banks where some sail out and some
sail in,
But which among them know what partings mean?

Your tears flowing free,
My tears flowing free,
Even with hearts that beat as one, betrothed we cannot be
Already the tide runs deep in the estuary!

CHANG HSIEN

(A.D. 990–1078)

Chang Hsien was a native of Wu-hsing in Chekiang Province, and passed the literary doctorate examination of 'chin shih' into government service. He served on the Board of Punishments in the Sung capital, later going south to Hangchow where he seems to have lived a peripatetic existence.

As a poet he is not ranked among the greatest, but his verse has a certain charm and one critic called its flavour 'unusual and lasting'. An example of this is given here in Poem 12 where, to make his effect, he writes of 'the shadow-shape of a swing' without mentioning any more directly the swing itself, let alone the girl on it.

更漏子　　　　　　張　先

錦筵紅，羅幕翠，侍宴美人姝麗。十五六，解憐才，勸人深酒杯。　黛眉長，檀口小，耳畔向人輕道：柳陰曲，是兒家，門前紅杏花。

11

A festal cloth of red,
A silken screen of blue;
A pretty girl is waiting gracefully on you.
Aged fifteen or sixteen,
Her understanding skill
Persuades the guests to fill and to refill.

Long pencilled brows of jet,
Small sandal-scented mouth
Close beside you whispering softly in your ear,
'Where the shady willows run
My house is the one
With an apricot blossoming red in front of the door.'

青門引　　　　張先

乍暖還輕冷，風雨晚來方定。庭軒寂寞近清明，殘花中酒，又是去年病。樓頭畫角風吹醒，入夜重門靜。那堪更被明月，隔牆送過秋千影！

12

P'u – Ch'ing Mên Yin
(*To the tune-title 'Song of the Green Gate'*)

Suddenly it's warm although the cold is threatening still
And the squally showers only stopped as evening fell.
Silence grips the courtyard now as Ch'ing-ming time
approaches.
The flowers are drooping. Deep in wine
I find my last year's grief is back again.

A bugle wind-borne from the watch-tower wakens me.
Night's fallen; the many doors stare silently.
How can I bear yet again what the shining moon will bring
As over the courtyard wall it sends the shadow-shape of a
swing!

YEN SHU

(A.D. 991–1055)

Yen Shu was one of the leading lyric writers of the (Northern) Sung Dynasty. The poem selected here, though not always quoted in Chinese anthologies, reads particularly true to life. The singing-girl occupied a prominent place in the life of the times and far from meaning simply a prostitute, included a very wide range of entertainers. They were educated to the point of being able to understand and sing the lyrics of the time, and the best were sought after by the highest in the land. A famous girl who lived about this time, Hua Kuei-nü, was courted by the whole country from the ruler downwards. But though she entertained them she would have nothing further to do with them and ended up by marrying a poor oil peddler whose annual income was said to be just about sufficient to purchase an evening's worth of his wife's 'official' company.

This particular lyric by Yen Shu will find an echo, later in this collection, in Po Chü-i's 'Song of a Guitar' (p. 205).

山亭柳　　　　晏　殊

家住西秦，賭薄藝隨身。花柳上，鬥尖新。偶學念奴聲調，有時高過行雲。蜀錦纏頭無數，不負辛勤。

數年來往咸京道，殘盃冷炙謾消魂。衷腸事，託何人？若有知音見採，不辭徧唱陽春。一曲當筵落淚，重掩羅巾。

13

P'u – Shan T'ing Liu
(To the tune-title 'Willows at the Hill Pavilion')

THE SINGING-GIRL

She had come from her home in Western Ch'in
And used her slender skill to make a living.
When it came to the songs of spring
She was quick with the latest hits.
She borrowed at times from the delicate style of Nien-nu;
At others she soared so high the clouds would pause in
passing.
With scarves of silk from Shu and liberal song money
Her work was well rewarded.

Then for several years she travelled the roads about the
capital;
A life of scraps and dirty cups, of shame that breaks the
spirit.
In whom could she confide
Her trouble-burdened heart?
If someone blessed with an ear for music enjoyed her
singing
She wouldn't refuse the difficult 'Yang Ch'un' song right
through.
One of the songs she sang that night so troubled her
She covered her face to hide her tears.

OU-YANG HSIU

(A.D. 1007–1072)

Ou-yang Hsiu's family, originally northerners, was one of the many which migrated south to the latitude of the Yangtze valley in the troubled times which beset the country towards the end of the T'ang Dynasty until the beginning of the Sung. He lost his father when he was only three years old but his widowed mother had the protection of a brother-in-law.

The young Ou-yang Hsiu applied himself with great diligence to his studies, and in A.D. 1030 he passed out top in the doctorate examination, and was posted to Loyang, the second capital of the country. There he established himself as a master of verse – and in particular of tz'u – and prose. It was at this time of his life that he spent much time enjoying the social rounds which included the night life of the city, and so earned a reputation which was to pursue him later in his career. But he was too lively and intelligent, and too devoid of humbug, to be set back by this, and his wide interests brought him more importantly into close contact with such forceful characters as Fan Chung-yen and the leading and young politicians and scholars of the day. What chiefly emerges from his writings – in the capital as well as in distant outposts when 'out of favour' – is his extraordinary fairmindedness and practical common sense, and his habit of getting to the root of a problem. His written views on the government entry examination system, and his attempts to introduce a greater liberty in the width of the subject-matter so as to lift the questions from being a pure exercise in memory of the classics, might have been written in this century. He rose to the highest positions in the state and has been acclaimed as one of the outstanding figures of the Sung Dynasty, as statesman, historian and writer.

In our earlier collection we included six of his tz'u. The little lyric translated here is a deceptively simple description of the onrush of spring in a climate where it arrives, delights and is gone in so short a space, leaving behind a parched earth. Fresh young grass and vigorous growth give way in the second verse to the hot sun's influence, spreading lassitude among the more elderly, a receptive languor in the young. The nesting season has arrived.

阮郎歸　　　　歐陽修

南園春半踏青時，風和聞馬嘶。青梅如豆柳如眉，日
長蝴蝶飛。花露重，草煙低，人家簾幕垂。秋千慵困解
羅衣，畫梁雙燕棲。

14

P'u – *Juan Lang Kuei*

SPRING IN THE SOUTH

Early spring in the southern gardens, a time to tread the
grass.
With a favouring wind you can hear the horses neigh.
Green plums the size of beans, willow-shoots like eyebrows.
Days lengthen, butterflies quiver.

Dew lies heavy on the flowers,
Mist hangs low on the grasses,
In houses blinds are hanging down.
Indolent girls on swings loosen their silken dresses.
On a painted beam a pair of swallows settle.

The poet Su Shih –
'The Cultured and Loyal Duke'

SU SHIH

(A.D. 1036–1101)

Su Shih, one of China's greatest poets (and more familiarly known as Su Tung-p'o) is more famous for his 'regular' verse (shih) than for his lyrics (tz'u). It is difficult though to over-estimate the influence he had on the development of the lyric as a verse-form. For the previous two centuries it had been accepted that the tz'u's proper sphere was the depicting of separation, nostalgia and other such heart-rending experiences. Su Shih cut adrift from this restriction, and with his interest in life, puckish humour and, on occasion, genuine feeling, used the tz'u for any subject that came into his head.

Bearing in mind the debt owed to Su Shih for setting the lyric free and for putting new vigour into it, it is amusing to read now a contemporary criticism (by Ch'ên Shih-tao, 1053–1101) of his tz'u. Su Shih's tz'u, Ch'ên wrote in all seriousness, were like Lei T'ai-shih, a famous director of the Imperial Dancing School (of girls). Unrivalled as Lei's skill was in dancing, to the extent that he was better than any of the girls, the fact remained that he was a man. Likewise Su Shih's lyrics, for all their excellence, were not 'of the natural colour', that is not the genuine article.

Su Shih was exiled to the far south of China in his later years for the political views he held. But he lived to see a change in policy at court which granted him freedom again though he died on his way back north. It was left to a later sovereign, the Emperor Hsiao-tsung, some sixty years after Su Shih's death, to grant him the posthumous title of Wen Chung Kung (Cultured and Loyal Duke) and the engraving opposite styles him as such; this engraving on a memorial tablet was cut comparatively recently – in A.D. 1845 – and has the attraction of showing Su Shih in his favourite 'country clothes' of bamboo-leaf rain-hat and straw sandals.

65

少年遊　　　蘇　軾

去年相送，餘杭門外，飛雪似楊花。今年春盡，楊花似雪，猶不見還家。對酒捲簾邀明月，風露透窗紗。恰似姮娥憐雙燕，分明照，畫梁斜。

15

P'u – Shao Nien Yu
(*To the tune-title 'Wanderings in Youth'*)

Last year I saw you off
Outside the Yü-hang gate;
Like willow-down the snow was flying then.
This year, though spring is over
And willow-down's like snow
Yet no one sees you coming home again.

With wine before me I roll up the curtain, bidding the
moonlight enter;
In through the window-gauze dank moisture streams.
It seems that Chang-O watches closely over that pair of
swallows
Lighting them up where the moon shines
Aslant on the painted beams.

瑞鷓鴣　　　　　蘇　軾

城頭月落尚啼烏。朱艦紅船早滿湖，鼓吹未容迎五馬，水雲先已漾雙鳧。映山黃帽螭頭舫，夾岸青烟鵲尾爐。老病逢春只思睡，獨求僧榻寄須臾。

16

P'u – Jui Chê Ku
(To the tune-title 'The Lucky Partridge')

'*Before dawn at the festival, I went down to the lake. The Prefect
had not arrived, but two magistrates were there.*'

The moon sinks under the city wall;
already the crows call;
And look, out early all over the lake
red boats large and small.
The band's not even begun to play its welcome to the Prefect,
But a pair of ducks have rippled the waters
there where the shore mists fall.

Brightening hills reveal yellow-capped
heads in the dragon-bow boat.
Burners with magpie-tail handles line
the shore; blue smoke ribbons float.
But here's my old trouble – a 'Welcome to Spring'
and I'm thinking of nothing but sleep.
I'll be off on my own to the priest with a plea
for the short-term use of his cot.

沁園春　　　　　　　蘇軾

孤館燈青，野店雞號，旅枕夢殘。漸月華收練，晨霜耿耿；雲山摛錦，朝露團團。世路無窮，勞生有限，似此區區長鮮歡。微吟罷，憑征鞍無語，往事千端。

當時共客長安，似二陸初來俱少年。有筆頭千字，胸中萬卷；致君堯舜，此事何難！用舍由時，行藏在我，袖手何妨閒處看。身長健，但優游卒歲，且鬥樽前。

17

TO MY BROTHER TZU-YU

A lonely, dimly-lighted inn;
A country post-house, cock-crow time;
A pillowed traveller's sleeping stops.
By slow degrees the moonlight thins away.
Frost of dawn begins to sparkle;
Clouds on hills are spread brocade;
Morning dew collects in drops.

Worldly paths run endless on,
But toiling lives have each their end
And, like this unimportant person, find that joy is rare.
I chanted verses awhile;
Then, as I leant in silence against my saddle,
In a thousand shapes the past was there.

That time we lived in the Capital together
Like the Lu brothers, newly arrived, both young,
Our brushes poised for a thousand words,
Our minds immersed in ten thousand scrolls.
Raising a ruler like Yao or Shun –
What difficulty lay in that?
To be used or dismissed depends on the times;
To proceed or withdraw is our own affair.
Hand in sleeve, why not watch, resigned?
As long as our bodies have vigour
We can do as we wish to the end of our days –
Like gaming over a jar of wine!

江城子　　　　　　　　蘇　軾

十年生死兩茫茫，不思量，自難忘。千里孤墳，無處話淒涼。縱使相逢應不識：塵滿面，鬢如霜。

夜來幽夢忽還鄉。小軒窗，正梳妝。相顧無言，唯有淚千行。料得年年腸斷處：明月夜，短松崗。

18

TO HIS DEAD WIFE

Ten years ago; one living, one long dead; what gulfs apart!
Though heedless of her, yet
I could not well forget
Those thousand miles to her lonely grave;
Too far to talk to her from a lonely heart.
But even could we meet each other, would she recognize
This face engraved with care,
The hoar-frost in my hair?

One night, sleeping alone, I dreamed I was suddenly home
again
At her little window; there
She was, combing her hair.
We looked at each other; we brought no words,
Only the many furrows of our tears.
Year after year I know my heart will visit that pitiful place
At night when the bright moon shines
On the hill with its stunted pines.

江城子　　　蘇　軾

老夫聊發少年狂：左牽黃，右擎蒼，錦帽貂裘，千騎卷平岡。為報傾城隨太守，親射虎，看孫郎。

酒酣胸膽尚開張。鬢微霜，又何妨！持節雲中，何日遣馮唐。會挽雕弓如滿月，西北望，射天狼。

19

P'u – Chiang Ch'êng Tzu
(To the tune-title 'The River by the City Wall')

OUT HUNTING AT MI-CHOU

The seasoned hunter off for the day to risk his life with the
young,
A hound at leash on my left arm,
A grizzled hawk on my right,
With embroidered hat and sable coat
Over the rolling hills I ride with the throng.
Crowds from the city follow their Prefect so that each can
say
'I saw him shoot the tiger,
I watched that old-time warrior!'

Buttressed well with wine I square my shoulders, play the
man.
These lightly frosted temples,
Of what consequence are they?
Once I served on the Emperor's Council;
When will someone lift the Imperial ban?
For I can bend the graven bow to the shape of the full moon
And keeping watch North-Westwards
Shoot the Wolf-Pack down!

照日深紅暖見魚。連村綠暗晚藏烏。黃童白叟聚睢盱。　麋鹿逢人雖未慣，猿猱聞鼓不須呼。歸來說與采桑姑。

旋抹紅妝看使君。三三五五棘籬門。相排踏破蒨羅裙。　老幼扶攜收麥社，烏鳶翔舞賽神村。道逢醉叟臥黃昏。

20

P'u – Wan Ch'i Sha
(To the tune-title 'Washing Silk by the Stream')

THANKSGIVING FOR RAIN

I

In the blood-red warmth of the sun's reflection basking
fish are seen.
Village by village the crows at twilight shelter in darkening
green.
The young men and their white-haired elders gather to
drink me in.

Shy as a deer uncertain still of every man it sees,
Prying as apes that come unbidden to any noise there is,
When they get back they will tell the girls out picking
mulberries.

II

Quickly rubbing on rouge they're ready to greet their
magistrate;
Scrambling all at sixes and sevens eagerly through the gate
They push and trample enough to tear the coloured silk of
a skirt.

To celebrate the harvest old and young walk hand in hand
In thanksgiving procession. Village kites go wheeling
round.
You meet old men in drunken sleep by the road at the day's end.

麻葉層層檾葉光。誰家煮繭一村香！隔籬嬌語絡絲娘。　垂白杖藜抬醉眼，捋青搗麨軟飢腸。問言豆葉幾時黃？

軟草平莎過雨新。輕沙走馬路無塵。何時收拾耦耕身？　日暖桑麻光似潑，風來蒿艾氣如薰。使君元是此中人。

III

Layer by layer and tier on tier the hemp-leaf gloss extends.
Which is the house that boils cocoons filling the village
with scents?
Voices of girls who reel the silk are floating over the fence.

Bent on a stick with upturned bleary eyes a hoary old
fellow
Rubs and pounds some grain to soothe his hunger rumbling
hollow.
Shall I ask him now to say when bean leaves will turn
yellow?

IV

After the rain the sedgy flats and bent grass look like new
As I ride my horse on the buoyant sand the dustless pathway
through.
When, I wonder, will the time come round to furbish up
my plough?

Warmed in the sun the rain-wet hemp and mulberry leaves
are glowing;
Wafting scent from over the fragrant herbs a wind is blowing.
Deep in this official's heart a peasant's blood is flowing.

浣溪沙　　　　蘇　軾

慚愧今年二麥豐。千歧細浪舞晴空。化工餘力染天紅。　　歸去山公應倒載，闌街拍手笑兒童。甚時名作錦薰籠。

21

P'u – Wan Ch'i Sha
(*To the tune-title 'Washing Silk by the Stream'*)

A vision seldom comes like this year's wheat and barley
harvest;
Rippling stalks in thousands dancing under a cloudless sky.
Into each young petal nature's vigour spreads her dye.

A village elder, gloriously drunk, is carted home;
Blocking the street the local youth clap hands and laugh
for joy.
How comes the scented daphne to be shaped so exquisitely?

定風波　　　蘇軾

莫聽穿林打葉聲。何妨吟嘯且徐行。竹杖芒鞋輕勝馬，誰怕！一莎烟雨任平生。　　料峭春風吹酒醒，微冷。山頭斜照却相迎。回首向來蕭瑟處，歸去：也無風雨也無晴。

22

P'u – Ting Fêng P'o

CALM AFTER THE STORM

Don't listen to that sound of drumming on the forest leaves;
Why not boom and bellow as you make your way at leisure?
Grass sandals and a bamboo staff are better than a horse;
Who's afraid?
In mist and rain a straw-plait cape is worth a lifetime's
pleasure.

The rough spring wind awakens me and blows away the wine;
It grows chill.
But here's the setting sun in welcome as we crest the hill.
I turn my head – how lonely, bleak and desolate down
there!
And so back home
To life unlike the weather's fair to foul and foul to fair.

浣溪沙　　　　蘇　軾

山下蘭芽短浸溪。松間沙路淨無泥。蕭蕭暮雨子規啼。　　誰道人生無再少？門前流水尚能西。休將白髮唱黃雞！

23

P'u – Wan Ch'i Sha
(*To the tune-title 'Washing Silk by the Stream'*)

Under the hill in the flooding stream the short-stemmed
orchids lie;
Under the scatter of pines the sandy pathway's fresh and dry;
The sighing sound of rain at evening blends with the night-jar's
cry.

Who has decreed that man can never regain his youth gone
by?
Look at that river beyond the gateway, flowing towards
the west!
Don't, whenever the yellow cock crows, fret that the
seasons fly.

臨江仙　　　　蘇軾

夜飲東坡醒復醉，歸來彷彿三更。家童鼻息已雷鳴。敲門都不應，倚杖聽江聲。　長恨此身非我有，何時忘却營營？夜闌風靜縠紋平。小舟從此逝，江海寄餘生。

24

P'u – Lin Chiang Hsien
(*To the tune-title 'The Immortal by the River'*)

Sobering up from an evening's drinking at Tung-p'o I got
drunk again
And reached my home at the third watch or somewhere
around.
The boy who helps me about the house was snoring like
thunder; my call
And knocks on the door produced no answer at all.
I leant on my stick, alive to the river's sound.

I have long regretted the way I live and my lack of control
of it.
When shall I shake off such feverish memories?
Late on a windless night, a sheet of unrippled silk for river,
To sail away in a small boat for ever,
Life unfolding on distant rivers and seas.

蝶戀花　　　蘇軾

花褪殘紅青杏小。燕子飛時，綠水人家繞。枝上柳綿吹又少。天涯何處無芳草！

牆裏秋千牆外道。牆外行人，牆裏佳人笑。笑漸不聞聲漸悄。多情却被無情惱。

25

P'u – Tieh Lien Hua
(*To the tune-title 'Butterflies Courting the Flowers'*)

Faded blossom, withered petals, small green apricots;
Time when swallows dip across
The green of water winding through the village.
Blown away from branches, dwindling willow floss;
Everywhere in sight springing grass.

Inside the wall a swing, outside a road.
Outside the wall a passer-by;
Inside a girl, a pretty girl who laughs . . .
The laughter fades; one by one other noises die.
Love, left without response, nurses injury.

CH'IN KUAN

(A.D. 1049–1100)

Ch'in Kuan was one of four brilliant students of the great poet
Su Shih, and wrote with both feeling and technical skill. He
had the facility, too, of establishing in his verse an atmosphere,
with clarity and economy of words. But Ch'in Kuan was not
always guiltless of over-elaboration and the story is told of Su
Shih meeting him one day and asking if he had been writing any
lyrics. Ch'in Kuan, clearly proud of being able to trot out an
example of note, quoted two lines, of a total of thirteen some-
what high-flown characters (which might be translated literally
'below the verandah connecting the small storeyed buildings I
saw a fleet horse, with decorated trappings and carved saddle').
Su Shih's comment was 'Thirteen characters! and all you've
said is "A man riding a horse has passed by the house"'.

The theme of Poem 26 is – as the name of the tune-title implies –
the legend of the Weaver-Girl (the star we know as Vega) and
the Herd-Boy (the star Aquila), a theme much used in poetry,
of which Ch'in Kuan's is probably the best of the verses.

The legend has it that the Sun God, finding his daughter too
preoccupied with her loom, thought he should marry her off
to a neighbouring young man – a herd-boy. But no sooner were
they married than the weaver-girl stopped all work and became
thoroughly irresponsible. The Sun God attributed this to the
herd-boy, to whom she was devoted, and in a fury banished her
to the other side of the Milky Way; but he agreed to his daughter
visiting her husband once a year, on the seventh night of the
seventh moon. For the trip he arranged that she should be
carried there and back on a bridge formed by the wings of
thousands of magpies.

鵲橋仙　　　秦　觀

纖雲弄巧，飛星傳恨，銀漢迢迢暗度。金風玉露一相逢，便勝卻人間無數。　柔情似水，佳期如夢，忍顧鵲橋歸路？兩情若是久長時，又豈在朝朝暮暮！

26

P'u – Ch'üeh Ch'iao Hsien
(To the tune-title 'Immortals of the Magpie Bridge')

THE WEAVER-GIRL AND THE HERD-BOY

As lovely clouds contrive new patterns
These flying stars fulfil their yearnings,
In darkness crossing the distant gulf of the Milky Way.
What though they only meet in the Golden Wind and the
Pearly Dew?
They are happier far than the countless people living on
earth.

Her gentle heart is soft as water,
The blissful hours flow like a dream.
Of the journey back by the Magpie Bridge can they bear a
thought?
When feelings stir in the hearts of lovers deeper than time's
abyss
Does it matter how seldom they meet?

望海潮　　　　　秦　觀

梅英疏淡，冰澌溶洩，東風暗換年華。金谷俊游，銅駝巷陌，新晴細履平沙。長記誤隨車；正絮翻蝶舞，芳思交加，柳下桃蹊，亂分春色到人家。　西園夜飲鳴笳。有華燈礙月，飛蓋妨花。蘭苑未空，行人漸老，重來是事堪嗟。煙暝酒旗斜。但倚樓極目，時見棲鴉。無奈歸心，暗隨流水到天涯。

27

P'u – Wang Hai Ch'ao
(*To the tune-title 'Watching the Tides'*)

Though scarce the plum and frail its scent
The ice breaks up, drifts slowly by
As east winds imperceptibly change the season.
We used to stroll in the Golden Valley garden
Or down the gay Bronze Camel street
And trod the sanded road as soon as the storms had passed.
I shall always remember straying to follow the carriages
At the time of willow-down flight and butterfly dances;
The season's pleasures enfolded me.
On the alley of peaches, under the willows,
Many-sided spring arrived in the homes of men.

There was drinking and music then in the Western Garden
at night;
Painted lamps outshone the moon,
Carriages hid the flowers from sight.
Now others bask in pride of office.
I'm just a traveller growing old
And all I do, returning here, is fret and sigh.
A vintner's sign in the night-mist, hanging awry.
Yet still I lean from the balcony, gazing abroad
As home to roost the crows flap by.
Nothing remains except to withdraw;
Dreams of the past flow on with the waters over the edge
of the sky.

HO CHU

(about A.D. 1063–1120)

Ho Chu came of a family from the town now known as Shao-hsing in Chê-kiang, famous for its rice wine. Quixotic in temperament and argumentative, he liked to discuss the affairs of the world. He first became a military official but later changed to the civil side, retiring finally to Soochow, not his native town but also in the southern part of the country.

The poem selected for inclusion in this collection is written with a background familiar to anyone who has moved on the water-ways of China, carrying as they have done over the ages the great bulk of the travelling population and transported goods. On this occasion there is perhaps a ferry-boat, filled with the usual assortment of passengers, with a young woman pushing a creaking oar in the stern, and, maybe, a child leaning on her mother for support. The poet, with his sympathies clear enough, sets himself to wondering. (See Notes on Poems, p. 245, for a different interpretation.)

生查子　賀鑄

西津海鶻舟　徑度滄
江雨雙艣本無情鶂
軋如人語　揮金陌上
郎化石山頭婦何物
繫君心三歲扶牀女

28

P'u – Shêng Ch'a Tzu
(*To the tune-title 'The Flowering Quince'*)

THE FERRY BOAT

On the western creek a hawk-swift boat
Crosses the river grey with rain.
Its pair of oars can have no feeling
Yet croak and mutter like gossips talking.

A husband sows his path with gold;
Staunch on a hill a wife is turned to stone.
What is it makes this heart so anxious?
A girl of two who can't quite stand alone.

LI CHIH I

(about A.D. 1090)

Li Chih-i was born in the province of Shantung. He passed his
doctorate (chin-shih) into Government service in A.D. 1082 and
at one time served, at Ting-chou, as one of Su Shih's assistants
and was highly thought of by him. He was best known as a
prose writer, but critics have commented on the conciseness of
his tz'u, ranking him in the same class as, though below, Ch'in
Kuan. As so often happened, Li Chih-i ran into trouble when
Su, his 'patron', fell out of favour with the Palace.

The verse selected here is written in the style of the old folk-
songs, if it is not actually based on one.

卜算子　　　　　李之儀

我住長江頭，君住長江尾。日日思君不見君，共飲長江水。　此水幾時休，此恨何時已。只願君心似我心，定不負相思意。

29

I live at the head of the Great River,
    You live at the Great River's tail.
Daily I think of you; though I don't see you
    Both of us drink from the Great River.

When will these waters fail?
    When will these longings end?
I have one wish; that your heart and my heart
    Stay true to love's bond.

THE SIXTEEN-CHARACTER SHORT LYRIC
(*Shih-liu-tzu Ling*)

his extremely short pattern of verse is likely to have been one
f the early transitional forms of the tz'u in its development from
ıe traditional shih. It has been known by two other names
ɔsides the obvious one describing the numbers of characters
.e. words) in its pattern; one was 'Ts'ang-wu Yao' ('The Ballad
f the Phoenix Tree'), and the other 'Kuei-tzu Yao', so called
om the character 'Kuei' with which it started. 'Kuei' meant
eturn' in the sense of 'return to one's native place' and this was
ı effect therefore a send-off verse for someone who was going
ɔme. A typical example of this form, by the poet Chang
[siao-hsiang (A.D. 1132–1169), seeing off a high government
fficial, reads

Homeward!
Gently the warm breezes your embroidered banner swell.
But let me keep you still
To raise once more a wine-cup in farewell.

Both alternative names of the sixteen-character lyric use the
ord 'Yao' – that is a ballad, folk-song, or popular song – which
ves a clue to its origin. In spite of its brevity it will be seen to
ive a near-colloquial turn of phrase and not to be as epigram-
atic as it might well have been. The pattern of the verse –
– 7 – 3 – 5 characters in the four lines, making a total of
xteen – was regarded as the correct one, rather than the form
ɔmetimes used starting with a line of three characters.

十六字令　　　　　周邦彦

眠！月影穿窗白玉錢。無人弄，移過枕函邊。

十六字令　蒼梧謠　　蔡　伸

天！休使圓蟾照客眠。人何在？桂影自嬋娟。

30

CHOU PANG YEN
(A.D. 1057–1121)

P'u – Shih Liu Tzu Ling
(*To the tune-title 'The Sixteen-Character Short Lyric'*)

TO THE MOON

Repose!
Moonlight through my window stipples in white jade shadows.
Nobody guides them on
As sidling past my pillow they are gone.

31

TS'AI SHÊN
(About A.D. 1100)

P'u – Shih Liu Tzu Ling
(*To the tune-title 'The Sixteen-Character Short Lyric'*)

Heaven,
Stop the full moon shining on this sleep-starved traveller!
Where can my lover be?
The moon's beauty is wasting itself on me.

清萬里關山共月明難禁受夜二擣衣聲

十六字令　旅思　陳見鑣

32

CH'ÊN CHIEN LUNG

The 'pounding on the washing stone', the thud, down by the water's edge, of the wooden mallet on clothes as they were beaten clean, to be dried the next morning, is one of the most nostalgic noises in China, and is frequently referred to by poets.

Chinese also remember that one of the great beauties of their stories of the past, Hsi Shih, washed clothes for a livelihood by a river of Yüeh. The ruler of Yüeh presented her to the King of Wu so that he should become so infatuated that he would be unable to devote any attention to the protection of his state. Girls tried, unsuccessfully, to copy her frowns as they were part of her entrancing loveliness. (See Wang Wei's poem, translated by Soame Jenyns in *A Further Selection from the 300 Poems of the T'ang Dynasty*, published by John Murray.)

P'u – Shih Liu Tzu Ling
(*To the tune-title 'The Sixteen-Character Short Lyric'*)

So clear,
Ten thousand miles of countryside sharing the same bright moon.
The pain is hard to bear –
Nightly, that pounding on the washing stone.

Southern Sung Dynasty

YÜEH FEI

(A.D. 1102–1141)

Few of the lyrics written by this great soldier have come down to us. The one most well known and quoted, which reveals his pent-up fury and frustration at not being allowed to resume his campaigns in the field against the Chin Tartars, we have already printed in our first collection. We reproduce, on p. 246, an engraving of Yüeh Fei's own calligraphy of this tz'u, the translation being printed for convenience in 'Notes on Poems' opposite it.

A second poem, included in this collection, is interesting in that it was written from the same pagoda at Wu-ch'ang on the Yangtze River on which Mao Tse-tung, early in his career, wrote his verse 'The Yellow Crane Tower'. The tower with its commanding view over the countryside was said to mark the place where Tzu-an, a Taoist recluse, having changed into an immortal had alighted from the yellow crane on which he was riding on his way to the Taoist heaven.

滿江紅　　　　岳　飛

遙望中原荒煙外，許多城郭。想當年花遮柳護，鳳樓龍閣。萬歲山前珠翠繞，蓬壺殿裏笙歌作。到而今，鐵騎滿郊畿，風塵惡。

兵安在，膏鋒鍔。民安在，填溝壑。歎江山如故，千村寥落。何日請纓提銳旅，一鞭直渡清河洛。却歸來，再續漢陽遊，騎黃鶴。

33

THE YELLOW CRANE TOWER

In the distance, look; beyond the spreading mists to the
    central Plain –
How many cities once there were!
Think back along those years and there,
  encircled by blossom and willow,
Stood Phoenix Tower and Dragon Hall.
On the face of Wan-sui-shan
  painted railings wound along;
In the P'eng-hu-tien
  music sounded, pipe and song.
But now
In the Imperial City's suburbs armoured horsemen throng,
Raising a foul dust.

Our soldiers, where are they?
Grease for the tips of lances.
Our people, where are they?
Choking up the ditches.
For alas! although the rivers and hills remain
Villages in thousands lie forsaken.
When can I offer to lead a mighty army
In one resistless sweep across the land of the great rivers?
And then come back again
To Han-Yang, and there take up my freedom – an Immortal
Riding his Yellow Crane.

CHU TUN JU

(about A.D. 1080–1175)

Chu Tun-ju was a native of Lo-yang (now known as Honan-fu). When the Tartars in 1126 invaded the north and captured Lo-yang, then the Sung Dynasty's second capital city, he fled to the far south – Kwangsi and Kwangtung – like so many of the literati of the time.

He was slow in going into government service, preferring his freedom, but eventually took office under Ch'in Kuei, the Sung Dynasty Prime Minister who followed a policy of appeasement with the Tartars. Ch'in Kuei was anathematized generally for his policy and in particular for his hand in the poisoning of the great patriotic general, Yüeh Fei. As was to be expected Chu Tun-ju's connection with Ch'in Kuei has not added to his reputation.

It is interesting to compare the following lyric with Poem No. 2 in this book, by Chang Chih-ho, written some three hundred and fifty years earlier. The earlier verse, which the great Su Shih tried to improve upon and failed, has the more direct appeal. The reader may feel that Chang Chih-ho had himself fished in all weathers; whereas Chu Tun-ju was more of an amateur observing the fisherman's conditions of life and surroundings with a keen eye but with philosophical detachment.

搖首出紅塵，醒醉更無時節。生計綠蓑青笠，

慣披霜衝雪。

晚來風定釣絲閒，上下是新月。

千里水天一色，看孤鴻明滅。

撥轉釣魚船，江海儘為吾宅。恰向洞庭沽酒，

却錢塘橫笛。

醉顏禁冷更添紅，潮落下前磧。

經過子陵灘畔，得梅花消息。

34

P'u – Hao Shih Chin
(To the tune-title 'Joys Approaching')

THE FISHERMAN

I

Turning away from cares of earth
Sober or drunk I let all time's conventions go.
I do my work in a green straw cape and a bamboo hat;
And coats I wear, of frost and driving snow.

Evening comes, the wind has died, hook and line hang idle;
Over and under me shines the new moon.
As endless miles of water and sky are merged together
A lonely swan shows clear but is quenched soon.

II

When I take out my fishing boat
All the rivers and seas are home to me wherever
I go, one moment laying in wine by the Tung-t'ing lake,
At another, playing the flute by the Ch'ien-t'ang river.

Inflamed with wine to check the cold my face grows redder
still.
Down rocks awash the ebbing stream descends;
And now we've passed the Tzu-ling sand-bank and are clear
I must put in for news about my friends.

短棹釣魚船，江上晚煙籠碧。塞雁海鷗分路，

占江天秋色。　錦鱗潑剌滿籃魚，取酒價相敵。

風順片帆歸去，有何人留得？

猛向這邊來，得個信音端的。天與一輪釣線，

領煙波千億。　紅塵今古轉船頭，鷗鷺已陳跡。

不受世間拘束，任東西南北。

III

I guide my boat with a shortened oar;
Evening mist on the river spreads a cloak of green.
The gulls and migrant geese, flying their separate ways,
Command the autumnal scene.

A sparkling glitter of flapping scales, a basketful of fish
To be changed for wine, whatever their worth may be.
Then with a favouring wind I'll set all sail and return,
And who's to hinder me?

IV

A sudden urge to cross the lake!
I knew the fish were there from every sign they gave.
And now this single line is stretching from the sky
As though it held the weight of mist and wave.

Earthly cares, the new and old, are like a boat-head's
veerings,
Or gull's or heron's flight, no traces show.
I was never subject to a world that would confine me;
East, west, south, north, I am free to go.

K'ANG YÜ CHIH

(about A.D. 1140)

K'ang Yü-chih, like Chu Tun-ju, served under Ch'in Kuei (see p. 117), and became one of his most important confidants.

He was dismissed and imprisoned after Ch'in Kuei's death, though he managed to emerge later.

His own collection of his poems no longer exists but some of them were found and published by Chao Wan-li.

采桑子〔醜奴兒令〕　　康與之

馮夷剪碎澄溪練，飛下同雲。著地無痕。柳絮
梅花處處春。　山陰此夜明如畫，月滿前村。莫
掩溪門。恐有扁舟乘興人。

35

P'u – Ts'ai Sang Tzu (Ch'ou Nu Erh Ling)
(*To the tune-title 'Picking Mulberries'*)

IN PRAISE OF SNOW

Feng I's scissors are snipping morsels of white off a silken
stream:
Flying down in clouds they come;
They touch the ground, no stains appear.
It's willow-down, it's plum-blossom, it's springtime
everywhere!

It's bright as day tonight on the northern side of the hill;
Moonlight floods the village wall.
Leave the river gate un-shut,
People may be coming to enjoy the scene by boat.

FAN CH'ÊNG TA

(A.D. 1126–1193)

In 1126, the year that Fan Ch'êng-ta was born, the Sung Dynasty capital of Pien-liang (now K'ai-feng) fell to the Chin Tartars, and the Court fled south to set up their new capital, a few years later, in Hangchow. Fan Ch'êng-ta was a native of Wu-hsien (now Soochow in Kiangsu Province) so was himself already living south of the territory occupied by the Tartars.

He grew up to be a military governor, poet, historian and naturalist. He was greatly struck by the young Chiang K'uei's (see p. 163) literary and musical ability and presented him with one of the girls of his household. It is to Chiang K'uei that we owe a special poem dedicated to his benefactor, 'The Immortal of the Stone Lake'. Chiang K'uei writes:

. . . .
What are riches and honours to him but superficialities?
He liked the fragrance of green wine and the dancing of the
  lotus flowers
. . . . . .
. . . . . .
At Lu-kou he used to pull up his horse
And, in a moment of leisure, compose elegant verses about
  the chrysanthemums.
It is said that the barbarians
Learnt to imitate his headgear . . . .

Fan Ch'êng-ta does not seem to have been able to express in his lyrics the same individual character that emerges from his regular poetry (shih), which include scenes of country life, and from his prose accounts of his extensive travels as an official; the tz'u translated here is an example of 'elegant' verse without much punch.

憶秦娥　　　范成大

樓陰缺，闌干影臥東廂月。東廂月，一天風露，杏花如雪。

隔煙催漏金蚪咽，羅幃黯淡燈花結。燈花結，片時春夢，江南天闊。

36

P'u – I Ch'in O
(*To the tune-title 'Memories of a Girl of Ch'in'*)

The shade has cleared the tower
And the railing's shadow falling spreads from the moonlit
eastern room,
The moonlit eastern room.
A windy moisture laden sky;
Like snow, the apricot in bloom.

A blur of mist; the brazen spout of a water-clock speeds
the hour.
Will the lamp-wick threads, in the curtained gloom, spell
out a message for me,
Spell out a message for me?
I dreamed a little while of spring –
But how distant are the skies of the South Country!

LU YU

(A.D. 1125–1210)

Lu Yu was a tremendously prolific writer, and much of his verse is interesting in describing the everyday life of the times – a lantern festival, a flower seller, doctors and medicine in the village, service on the frontier and so on. But a good deal also is coloured by a self-pity which partly obscures a pleasant character, sensitive to the feelings and problems of the village community. The fact is that he was a disappointed man. He was upset first by his mother making him divorce the girl he had married and with whom he was deeply in love, and later by not being able to fight on the frontier against the Chin Tartars who were occupying the northern part of China. When he did manage to get north with the Army in the role of a civilian assistant the fighting was over and he became bored and overwrought – to use his own words. He is apt too often to try to build himself up into more of a he-man than the facts really justify – for example:

'Feathered arrows and carved bow;
What memories of calling up my falcon on the ruined ramparts
And of killing a tiger on the flat plain.'

or

'In the lantern light we would throw ourselves into the game,
And in carved saddle let fly our arrows at the gallop;
But who remembers the martial deeds of those years?'

This undercurrent is evident in both the poems which follow, but the point must not be driven too hard for Lu Yu was a poet of high standing and in much of his verse, amongst the extraordinary quantity of some 10,000 poems he has left us, his natural charm and power of description are unspoilt.

131

卜算子　　　　陸　游

驛外斷橋邊，寂寞開無主。已是黃昏獨自愁，更著風和雨。　　無意苦爭春，一任羣芳妒。零落成泥碾作塵，只有香如故。

37

P'u – Pu Suan Tzu
(To the tune-title 'The Fortune-Teller')

IN PRAISE OF PLUM BLOSSOM

Outside the post-house by a broken bridge
Solitary and unremarked it flowers;
Melancholy, alone in the twilight
Or buffeted by squally showers;

Never presuming to rival spring's colours,
Unmoved when others mass round it enviously.
Its petals fall to earth, are trampled to dust;
A fragrant memory.

訴衷情　　　　陸　游

當年萬里覓封侯，匹馬戍梁州。關河夢斷何處，塵暗舊貂裘。胡未滅，鬢先秋，淚空流。此生誰料，心在天山，身老滄洲。

38

P'u – Su Chung Ch'ing
(*To the tune-title 'Telling one's True Feelings'*)

I marched ten thousand miles that year, serving my
country
In charge of the frontier post at Liang-chou.
That life of river and pass has faded like a dream.
Dust greys my sables of long ago.

The Tartars were not broken;
Autumn has tinged my temples.
Tears vainly flow.
Who could guess I would end this life
My heart far off in the T'ien Shan,
My worn-out body in Ts'ang-chou?

HSIN CH'I CHI
(A.D. 1140–1207)

'he Southern Sung poets make continual reference to their lost
erritories. This amounted to an obsession with soldiers and
cholars like Yüeh Fei, Lu Yu and Hsin Ch'i-chi, but it is
ardly surprising considering that they had just lost half their
ountry – and that half containing the capital with all its national
ssociations – to a foreign 'barbarian' enemy. As a younger
nan Hsin Ch'i-chi had seen active service against the invader
nd, like Yüeh Fei, had no doubts that this enemy could be
jected if only the Government had the backbone and resolu-
ion.

Hsin Ch'i-chi's verse in these circumstances, while not without
ts note of despair in his nostalgia, is virile and wide-ranging,
nd he remains with Li Yü (the Southern T'ang ruler) and Su
hih one of the great architects of the lyric. Unlike these other
wo, but like Liu Yung (about A.D. 1045) and Chou Pang-yen
A.D. 1057–1121), Hsin Ch'i-chi wrote exclusively in the tz'u
erse-form.

Poems in this collection such as Nos 42, 44 and 47 illustrate
is natural pleasure in the life around him contrasting in their
implicity with Nos 49 and 50 ('Dragon Pool'), so full of allusion
hat without the notes in Appendix 1 much of the contents
vould be incomprehensible to the general reader. The second
erse of No. 50, however, and particularly the last six lines, have
he poignancy of all deeply felt experience distilled by a true
oet into simple words – in this case, of peace and resignation.

生查子　　　　　　辛棄疾

去年燕子來，繡戶深深處，花徑得泥歸，都把琴書污。　今年燕子來，誰聽呢喃語？不見捲簾人，一陣黃昏雨。

39

P'u – Shêng Ch'a Tzu
(*To the tune-title 'The Flowering Quince'*)

THE EMBROIDERY ROOM

Last year when the swallows came
Deep inside the embroidery room they flew,
Bringing clay from pathways laid with petals,
Fouling books and lute each time anew.

This year when the swallows came
No one listened to their twittering cries.
Nobody's been seen to draw the curtain.
Twilight brings a gust of rain as it dies.

生查子　　　　辛棄疾

悠悠萬世功，砣砣當年苦。魚自入深淵，人自居平土。　　紅日又西沉，白浪長東去。不是望金山，我自思量禹。

40

P'u – Shêng Ch'a Tzu
(To the tune-title 'The Flowering Quince')

IN PRAISE OF THE GREAT ENGINEER – THE EMPEROR YÜ

His mighty works outlast the ages.
His bitter years of unremitting labour
Gave fish their entry to the deep waters,
Man his home on the plains.

A red sun sinks to the west once more;
White waves flow to the east as ever.
My gaze is not for the Golden Isle;
I am thinking only of the Great Yü.

菩薩蠻　　　辛棄疾

鬱孤臺下清江水，中間多少行人淚。西北望長安，可憐無數山。青山遮不住，畢竟東流去。江晚正愁予，山深聞鷓鴣。

41

P'u – P'u Sa Man
(*To the tune-title 'The Strange Goddesses'*)

The waters of the Clear River run by Yü-ku-t'ai;
How many fugitives have filled the waters with their tears?
Looking towards Ch'ang-an north-westerly
I mourn it hidden by so many hills.

And yet that green hill fence has never checked
The waters flowing east at last.
Evening, the river; my heart with longing fills
Hearing the partridge call deep in the hills.

清平樂 辛棄疾

村居

茅簷低小溪上
青青草醉裏
吳音相媚好
白髮誰家翁
媼　大兒鋤
豆溪東
中兒正
織雞籠
最喜小
兒無賴
溪頭臥剝
蓮蓬

42

Beside the little reed-thatched hut
How green they look, the stream-fed grasses there!
Happy with wine, absorbed in each other, talking in southern
accents,
Who can they be, that elderly couple with whitening hair?

The eldest son is hoeing beans on the eastern bank;
The middle one is weaving a chicken basket of reeds:
The smallest one's the happiest, watching without a care
Others by the water-side splitting lotus seeds.

清平樂　　　　辛棄疾

遶牀飢鼠，蝙蝠翻燈舞。屋上松風吹急雨，破紙窗間自語。　平生塞北江南，歸來華髮蒼顏。布被秋宵夢覺，眼前萬里江山。

43

P'u – Ch'ing P'ing Lê
(*To the tune-title 'A Song of the Joys of Peace'*)

HOME AGAIN

Round my bed, hungry rats;
Round the lamp, whirling bats.
On to the roof from the pines the wind blows scurrying
rain;
Tattered paper chatters in every window.

I have spent my life on the frontier and south in Chiang-nan.
Now home again, white-haired and worn,
Awake under my cotton quilt this night of autumn
I see those countless miles of river and mountain.

西江月　　　　　　　辛棄疾

明月別枝驚鵲，清風半夜鳴蟬。稻花香裏說豐年，聽取蛙聲一片。七八箇星天外，兩三點雨山前。舊時茅店社林邊，路轉溪橋忽見。

44

P'u – Hsi Chiang Yüeh
(*To the tune-title 'Moon on the West River'*)

Bright moonlight on a sloping branch; a magpie wakens;
    A cool wind at the midnight hour; cicadas sound.
The rice ear's scent leads on to talk of abundant harvest.
    The noise of croaking frogs is everywhere around.

    Seven or eight clusters of stars in the heavens,
      Two or three showers of rain in the hills.
Long ago there used to be an inn beside that wood –
And it's suddenly there, where the bridge runs over the
      stream at the bend!

西江月　　　　辛棄疾

醉裏且貪歡笑，要愁那得工夫。近來始覺古人書，信著全無是處。　　昨夜松邊醉倒，問松我醉何如？只疑松動要來扶，以手推松曰去！

45

P'u – Hsi Chiang Yüeh
(To the tune-title 'Moon on the West River')

Now I'm drunk I long for pleasure;
Where's the time for melancholy?
I'm just learning from the classics
Faith in all they teach is folly.

Drunk last night I fell down near some
Pines and asked 'How drunk am I?'
Feeling one had moved to help me
I pushed it and said 'Go away!'

浪淘沙　　　　　　辛棄疾

身世酒杯中，萬事皆空。古來三五個英雄。雨打風吹，何處是漢殿秦宮？　夢入少年叢，歌舞匆匆。老僧夜半誤鳴鐘，驚起西窗眠不得，捲地西風。

46

P'u – Lang T'ao Sha
(To the tune-title 'The Waves Scouring the Sands')

All that I live for's in a glass of wine;
How empty grows this world of mine!
In days of old a few examples of heroic man
Withstood and triumphed over storm and stress, but now
where are
Ch'in palaces and halls of Han?

Through dreams of crowded life enjoyed when young,
Flurry and scurry of dance and song,
I heard an old priest strike his midnight bell, untimely
sound!
Startled I rose, approached the western window and slept
no more;
Autumn wind spun over the ground.

鷓鴣天　　　　　　　　辛棄疾

陌上柔桑破嫩芽，東鄰蠶種已生些。平岡細草
鳴黃犢，斜日寒林點暮鴉。　山遠近，路橫斜，
青旗沽酒有人家。城中桃李愁風雨，春在溪頭
薺菜花。

47

By field paths now the tender mulberry breaks into delicate
shoots
And already some of my easterly neighbour's silk-worm
eggs are hatched.
In the fresh young grass on the flattened top of a mound a
yellow calf lows.
The sunset etches the naked woods and the homing dots of
crows;
The distant hills and near,
The plaited pathways there,
The weathered sign on a vintner's shop and the many
houses about.
Inside the walls the peach and plum look poorly after the
winter,
But up at the head of the stream the spring has brought its
wild-flowers out!

破陣子　　　　　　　　　辛棄疾

醉裏挑燈看劍，夢回吹角連營。八百里分麾下炙，五十絃翻塞外聲，沙場秋點兵。

馬作的盧飛快，弓如霹靂弦驚。了卻君王天下事，贏得生前身後名，可憐白髮生。

48

THE FRONTIER

Moved by wine to examine my sword I trimmed the lamp.
Dreams arose from the past of barracks and bugles calling,
Of roasting commissariat oxen portioned out to the army,
Of lutes of fifty strings and sounds of martial music swelling,
    Of autumn on the desert front and troops parading.

Our horses sped as swiftly as 'The Black One' of Liu Pei.
Like thunder claps our bow-strings twanged enough to
    frighten.
We could have settled once and for all the Emperor's
    paramount troubles
And earned as well a life-long fame our deaths could only
    heighten;
    Alas! my hairs whiten.

木蘭花慢　　　　辛棄疾

可憐今夕月，向何處、去悠悠？是別有人間，
那邊才見，光景東頭。是天外空汗漫，但長風
浩浩送中秋。飛鏡無根誰繫？姮娥不嫁誰留？

謂經海底問無由。恍惚使人愁。怕萬里長鯨，
從橫觸破，玉殿瓊樓。蝦蟆故堪浴水，問云何
玉兔解沉浮？若道都齊無恙，云何漸漸如鈎？

49

P'u – Mu Lan Hua Man
(*To the tune-title 'The Magnolia, a long lyric'*)

ODE TO THE AUTUMN MOON

How much to be pitied, this evening's moon!
　　　　Where is it heading
　　　As far, far away it goes?
　　　Either another world of men
　　　　　Watches it when
　　　Out of the East it glows,
　　Or in outer space's
　　　　　　empty wide expanses
Long-drawn mighty winds sweep on
　　　　　　mid-autumn's moon.
Who can bind such a free-flying mirror?
　　Chang-O misses a husband to guard his own.

　　Some say it goes to the bed of the sea,
　　　　　　but answer there's none!
　　Human care is rooted in such confusion.
Should we then fear a myriad-mile long whale
　　　Will smash them, bursting upon
　　　Jade Palace and Jasper Tower?
But surely the Toad can swim like one!
Then I ask you, how will the Jade Hare solve
　　　　the problem whether to sink or float?
If you say there'll be no disaster,
Explain that gradual change to a sickle moon.

159

水龍吟　　　　　　　　　　　　　　辛棄疾

舉頭西北浮雲，倚天萬里須長劍。人言此地，
夜深長見，斗牛光燄。我覺山高，潭空水冷，
月明星淡。待燃犀下看，憑欄卻怕，風雷怒，
魚龍慘。　　峽束蒼江對起，過危樓、欲飛還歛
。元龍老矣，不妨高臥，冰壺涼簟。千古興亡，
百年悲笑，一時登覽。問何人、又卻片帆沙岸，
繫斜陽纜？

50

P'u – Shui Lung Yin

THE DRAGON POOL

Look north-west, up there where the clouds loom,
You'ld need a sword sky-long to sweep it clear.
People say that here
Deep in the night can often be seen
A dragon blade flash up to the stars.
And this must be the high hill
And the deep pool, its water cold
In the bright moon and starlight pale.
On the point of peering into the depths,
Just as I leaned on the edge I was seized with terror
Of wind's and thunder's rage,
Venom of fish and dragon.

The steep sides of the gorge restrain the dark green waters;
Past the dizzy tower
They long to fly but are pent in.
Must I, another old Yüan-lung,
Remain content to drowse my life away
With a frosted jug on a mat of cool bamboo?
The ancients met success and failure,
The centuries match our griefs and joys –
I understand it all in a flash;
And who it is
Furling his sail by a sandy bank
To moor in the setting sun.

CHIANG K'UEI

P'u-Hsing Hua T'ien Ying
(to the tune-title 'A Song after Drinking')

Lu szu ti fu Yüan-yang P'u. Hsiang T'ao-yeh tang shih huan tu.

Yu chiang ch'ou yen yü ch'un fêng. Tai ch'ü. I lan jao, kêng shao chu.

Chin—ling lu. Ying yin yen wu. Suan ch'ao shui chih jên tsui k'u.

Man t'ing fang ts'ao pu ch'êng kuei. Jih mu. Kêng i chou hsiang shen ch'u.

For verse see Poem 51, p. 167.

CHIANG K'UEI

(A.D. 1155–1229)

Chiang K'uei was both a musician – a player on string and wind instruments and a composer – and poet. While he composed many tunes for his own verse he was always on the look-out for interesting music which he would copy, perhaps from some lute-player or from old music books. Examples of his music are shown with his poetry here, and for this we are indebted to Dr Laurence Picken and to the Hungarian Studia Musicologica for permission to reprint these most interesting and tuneful examples of secular music written over 700 years ago.

In our notes about the development of the tz'u as a verse form, emphasis has been placed on the influence of foreign music on popular fancy in China in the T'ang Dynasty period (A.D. 618–907), an influence so great that it is recorded that of the ten classes of music taught in the Music School eight were non-Chinese.

But even after these importations and after the waves of invasions from across their north-western and northern frontiers, Chinese music was to retain strong elements of its individuality. As Laurence Picken has pointed out (in *The New Oxford History of Music*, Vol. I, p. 86, O.U.P., 1960), 'primitive characteristics of musical culture are often preserved with great tenacity by peoples otherwise at a high cultural level'. It is interesting therefore to find in the songs reprinted here (pp. 162–4) evidence – as he goes on to say – of the 'persistence in China proper . . . of the characteristic minor third pentatonic genus, with the fourth as the dominant melodic unit', that is evidence 'in musical terms of the vigour in her autochthonous culture. . . . ' (Readers who would like to pinpoint this evidence of 'Chinese-ness' will find, for instance, in the tune for Poem No. 51 intervals of descending fourths in the second measure – 'yeh tang' – and in the second stanza – 'ling lu', 'yen wu', 'shui

163

CHIANG K'UEI

P'u-Ch'ang T'ing Yüan Man
(*To the tune-title 'Unhappiness at the Rest-House, a long lyric'*)

Chien ch'ui chin chih t'ou hsiang hsü. Shih ch'u jên chia. Lü shên mên hu.

Yüan p'u yung hui. Mu fan ling luan hsiang ho hsü.

Yüeh jên to i. Shui tê szǔ ch'ang t'ing shu.

Shu jo yu ch'ing shih. Pu hui tê ch'ing ch'ing ju tz'ǔ.

Jih mu. Wang kao ch'êng pu chien. Chih chien luan shan wu shu.

Wei Lang ch'ü yeh. Tsên wang tê Yü — huan fên fu.

Ti i shih tsao tsao kuei lai. P'a Hung — o wu jên wei chu.

Suan k'ung yu ping tao. Nan chien li ch'ou ch'ien lü.

For verse see Poem 54, p. 173.

chih' – as well as the equivalent in the combination of minor thirds and major seconds. Notwithstanding the fact that these tunes use all seven notes, the five-note type of fourth-segments dominate the course of the melody still.)

Chiang K'uei's verse is of a graceful elegance, but it lacks substance behind the words, like his calligraphy which again lacked only inspiration to be outstanding. As one Chinese critic has put it, he has all the technique and style but reading his verse is 'like looking at flowers through a mist' – there is nothing much one can get hold of. Two notable exceptions, however, are the poems written to his bride-to-be and his lament on the city of Yangchow – Nos 62 and 63 in our earlier volume *A Collection of Chinese Lyrics*. The music for the former – to the tune 'An Hsiang' (Secret Fragrance) – is placed opposite the English version which has been reprinted, for convenience sake, in Appendix I, Notes on Poems, pp. 254–5.

What does emerge, however, is Chiang K'uei's charm of character. He was scholarly and of slender means, and a family man devoted to Red Blossom, the girl who was presented to him by his patron Fan Ch'êng-ta (see p. 127). In a poem about the New Year Festival (to the tune 'Chê Ku T'ien') he writes of his small son's attempts at writing Chinese characters – and turning out a result that looked more like the grotesquely ugly and ferocious gods whose pictures decorated the sideposts of the main gate; at the same festival he carries his little daughter on his shoulder to see the sights. He was always happy, too, visiting Fan Ch'êng-ta where he was especially welcome for the composing of new tunes, or verses to fit a tune already composed by a member of Fan's family. Whatever else is said about his verse it certainly has a distinctly pleasing musical quality.

杏花天影　　　　姜　夔

綠絲低拂鴛鴦浦，想桃葉當時喚渡。又將愁眼與春風，待去，倚蘭橈更少駐。

金陵路、鶯吟燕儛，算潮水知人最苦。滿汀芳草不成歸，日暮，更移舟向甚處？

51

P'u – Hsing Hua T'ien Ying*

'*In the winter of 1186 I left Mien-k'ou and on the second day
of the month was passing Chin-ling; here I looked north to Huai
and Ch'u countries. It was a windy and clear day and we set
sail in our small boat and rode easily on the water.*'

Dangling threads of green are brushing Lovers' Waterway.
I think of Peach Leaf calling for the ferry boat that day
And once again with saddened eyes I share the winds of spring.
Nearly away
I rest on my magnolia oars – one more brief stay.

Above the road to Chin-ling orioles pipe and swallows sway.
These tides, I reckon, know the depths of human misery.
From wild-flower banks so thickly spread I cannot bear to stray.
The close of day
And I must move my boat on yet again – which way?

* The music for this verse will be found on p. 162.

醉吟商　　　姜　夔

又正是春歸，細柳暗黃千縷，暮鴉啼處。夢逐金鞍去。一點芳心休訴，琵琶解語。

52

P'u – Tsui Yin Shang
(*To the tune-title 'A Song after Drinking'*)

Spring again – away it goes!
Willow-threads in thousands stealthily turn yellow.
Dusk, and caws from roosting crows.

Follow in dreams a saddle of gold,
But never say what's in your heart;
Your lute will spell the words untold.

Yu chêng shih   ch'un   kuei..   Hsi liu an   huang ch'ien   lü.

Mu   ya   t'i   ch'u.   Mêng   chu   chin   an ch'ü.

I   tien   fang   hsin   hsiu   su.   P'i   pa   chieh   yü.

玉梅令　　　　　姜　夔

疏疏雪片，散入溪南苑，春寒鎖、舊家亭館。有玉梅幾樹，背立怨東風，高花未吐，暗香已遠。　公來領略，梅花能勸，花長好、願公更健。便揉春為酒，翦雪作新詩，拼一日、繞花千轉。

53

P'u – Yü Mei Ling
*(To the tune-title 'Jade Plum Blossom, a short lyric')**

'A member of Fan Ch'êng-ta's (Shih-hu) family had composed this tune. As there were no words for it, I was called upon to write some. To the south of Shih-hu's cottage, on the other side of the river, there was a field called "Fan's Piece". The plum-blossom was out, and snow was falling; the bamboo courtyard was most peaceful. Shih-hu was too frightened of the cold to come out, so I wrote this to chaff him.'

A sprinkling of snowflakes
Scattered south of the stream on to Fan's Piece.
Cold spring had fastened on
The family's old pavilion.
There, jade-white, stood several plum-trees,
Backs to the east wind turned resentfully.
Although the topmost blossom had not burst free
Its delicate scent already floated afar.

Host, come out and enjoy the scene!
Doesn't the plum encourage you?
Splendid as blossom grows,
So may your strength renew!
Then come, we'll crush the spring for wine,
Create new verse from crumbling snows,
Or spend the whole day long
Where flowery pathways turn and twine.

* The music for this verse will be found on p. xiv.

長亭怨慢　　　姜夔

漸吹盡、枝頭香絮，是處人家，綠深門戶。遠浦縈回，暮帆零亂向何許。閱人多矣，誰得似長亭樹。樹若有情時，不會得青青如此。

日暮，望高城不見，只見亂山無數。韋郎去也，怎忘得玉環分付：第一是早早歸來，怕紅萼無人為主！算空有并刀，難剪離愁千縷。

54

P'u – Ch'ang T'ing Yüan Man
To the tune-title 'Unhappiness at the Rest House, a long lyric')*

Gradually from the branches
the scented willow down is blown,
And people's doorways everywhere
with green are deeply overgrown.
To and fro the river winds afar
And sails at evening scatter –
where will they have gone?
I have watched many a man pass by
But which of them has flourished like
the trees at ferry stages?
If they could feel as we do, trees
Would never grow in colour and
luxuriance like these.

Evening comes; I can no longer
discern the city wall:
I only see that jagged line
of hills innumerable.
When the poet Wei left home
How did he forget his
Jade Ring's exhortation?
First of all, to return as soon as he could
In case Red Flower be left without a master.
I reckon even a knife from Ping would do no good:
It is hard to cut those countless threads
of grief in separation.

* The music for this verse will be found on p. 164.

SHIH TA TSU

(about A.D. 1170–?)

ıih Ta-tsu was born in Pien-liang (now K'ai-feng) the capital
ʹ the Northern Sung Dynasty. Entering Government service
ɛ rose to serve as an assistant to Han T'o-chou, the Prime
Ɪinister, who relied greatly upon him. So close was he to his
ıief that he was warned by a friend that he would be in danger.
ı the event, when Han T'o-chou was disgraced, Shih Ta-tsu
ıffered the punishment of having his face branded, and was
so of course dismissed. He spent his last years in distressed
rcumstances.
  As a poet he has been singled out as exceptional in his
eatment of living things, and the nineteenth-century critic
ʹang Kuo-wei regards the tz'u we have selected for this
ıllection as second only, in this category, to Su Shih's tz'u in
ʹaise of the Willow (translated in our first volume).

雙雙燕　　　　史達祖

過春社了，度簾幕中間，去年塵冷。差池欲住，試入舊巢相並。還相雕梁藻井，又軟語商量不定。飄然快拂花梢，翠尾分開紅影。

芳徑，芹泥雨潤。愛貼地爭飛，競誇輕俊。紅樓歸晚，看足柳昏花暝。應自棲香正穩，便忘了天涯芳信。愁損翠黛雙蛾，日日畫闌獨憑。

55

IN PRAISE OF SWALLOWS

Spring's festival has passed
And round the screen and into the heart of the room
To last year's nests, dusty and cold,
On tilted wings, looking for lodging,
They jostle side by side to reach their nests of old;
Scrutinize carved beam and painted ceiling,
Twitter softly together in endless talk that has no outcome;
Float swiftly on air, brush the tips of the flowers:
Blue-black tail-shadows bar the red blossom.

By the scented path
To the rain-soaked reed-bed mud, and there
They strive to cling the closest to earth in flight,
Wrangling, boasting their grace in air.
And so back late to the red-beamed chamber:
They've searched enough by willow and flower in the fading
light.
But should they be settling down snugly together?
Have they forgotten a message, welcome news from far
away?
Her pencilled eye-brows quiver in grief.
She waits by the painted screen, alone, day after day.

LIU K'O CHUANG

(A.D. 1187–1269)

Liu K'o-chuang was a southerner from Fukien who finally rose
to be provincial judge there. His life spans the last years of the
Southern Sung Dynasty before its fall to the Mongols in 1276.

The poem selected here brings out well the life that a young
government official had to put up with, transferred from one
post to another and anywhere but to his home town, in the early
stages of his career and before he had achieved a reputation
good enough to earn him a place at the capital.

Liu K'o-chuang was a prolific writer. He found great difficulty
in later life in making both ends meet, and even turned a beggar
away from his own door – an event worthy of note in a man
with his background.

玉樓春　　　　　　　　劉克莊

年年躍馬長安市，客舍似家家似寄。青錢換酒
日無何，紅燭呼盧宵不寐。

易挑錦婦機中字
，難得玉人心下事。男兒西北有神州，莫滴水
西橋畔淚。

56

P'u – Yü Lou Ch'un
(*To the tune-title 'Spring in the Jade Tower'*)

Year by year on a frisky horse to the capital I would go
Until my lodgings grew like home and home like lodgings
grew.
I changed my cash for wine and when the day was idled
through
Awake all night I called the dice in the rich red candle glow.

It's easy enough to get a verse embroidered on silk for you,
But hard to learn if the inmost heart of a pretty girl is true.
And now that men to the far north-west have settled in
lands we lost
It's not for girls at the Water Bridge that you should be
grieving so.

WANG CH'ING HUI

(about A.D. 1260)

Wang Ch'ing-hui was a female member of the Southern Sung Imperial Palace household staff in Hangchow. She was occupying the position of Superintendent of Ceremonies of the women's quarters in the palace when the Mongols captured Hangchow in A.D. 1276, and from there she was taken north as a prisoner.

The poem in this collection is therefore a first-hand account, however brief, of a terrifying ride.

Wang Ch'ing-hui eventually became a Tao-ist nun.

滿江紅　　　　　　　　　王清惠

太液芙蓉，渾不似、舊時顏色。曾記得、春風雨露，玉樓金闕。名播蘭馨妃后裏，暈潮蓮臉君王側。忽一聲、鼙鼓揭天來，繁華歇。　龍虎散，風雲滅。千古恨，憑誰說？對山河百二，淚盈襟血。驛館夜驚塵土夢，宮車曉碾關山月。問姮娥、於我肯從容，同圓缺。

57

P'u – Man Chiang Hung
(*To the tune-title 'Sunset on the River'*)

JOURNEY INTO CAPTIVITY

Mimosa at T'ai-yeh
Cannot have the same
Colour as in those days of old
Remembered from a past
Of spring-time dew and wind and rain
In the Jade Tower and Palace of Gold.
My name among the royal ladies spread like orchid-scent;
A blushing, bashful lotus-flower the Sovereign's grace
befriended.
When suddenly a clamour
Of war-drums fit to startle heaven burst.
The gay life ended.

Dragon and Tiger fled,
Cloud and Wind were gone.
To share such depth of sorrow
Whom could I count upon?
Faced with the sight of all those rivers and mountains
Blood stained my dress, the tears fell so.
Each night at road-side inns I woke in terror from dreams
of travel;
Each dawn the palace carriages rolled through passes lit
by the moon.
I begged Ch'ang-O
In kindness to allow me to go with her
Wherever she might go.

CHIANG CHIEH

(about A.D. 1270)

Chiang Chieh passed his doctorate of 'chin-shih' into government service. On the collapse of the Southern Sung Dynasty, when the Mongols captured Hangchow, he retired and in spite of requests to continue in official service refused to serve under a foreign ruler. For this loyalty he has been much admired.

虞美人　　　　蔣　捷

少年聽雨歌樓上，紅燭昏羅帳。壯年聽雨客舟中，江闊雲低，斷雁叫西風。而今聽雨僧廬下，鬢已星星也。悲歡離合總無情，一任階前點滴到天明。

58

P'u – Yü Mei Jen
(*To the tune-title 'Yü, the Beautiful One'*)

With singing girls when I was young
I listened to the rain,
The candles flickering red
Outside the curtained bed.
By boat I travelled in my prime
And listened to the rain,
The river wide, the cloud banks low,
A lone goose calling in the west wind's blow.

And now inside a Buddhist cell
I listen to the rain,
The silver in my hairs
As numberless as stars.
Grief at parting, joy of greeting
Dispossess our peace;
So; let them be; let them run on
Like rain dripping down on the steps till dawn.

Ch'ing Dynasty

NA-LAN HSING-TÊ

(A.D. 1655–1685)

Na-lan Hsing-tê, as the style of his Chinese name would imply, was a Manchu, born shortly after the conquest of the empire by his northern countrymen. Brought up in Peking as a Guards officer in the Imperial Palace, he learnt Chinese from childhood and became one of the outstanding lyric-writers to emerge after the Sung dynasty. His verse tends to be over-filled with literary allusion, as had become common well before his day, and he was much occupied with a Palace love-affair. But he is at his best when writing on his trips to the frontier on military duty, capturing in a few words the atmosphere of mountain defile, roaring stream, and the tented grasslands of his native herdsmen.

如夢令　　　納蘭性德

萬帳穹廬人醉，星影搖搖欲墜。歸夢隔狼河，又被河聲攪碎。還睡，還睡。解道醒來無味。

59

P'u – Ju Mêng Ling
(*To the tune-title 'As in a Dream, a short lyric'*)

Ten thousand felted tents filled with exhausted men;
Flicker and fade of stars about to set.
I was travelling home and trapped by the Wolf River –
that dream;
And again the river's clamour has broken it!
Let me sleep on,
Let me sleep on;
Awake, I know the savour of life will be gone.

Republic

CH'ENG HSI

(A.D. 1919–   )

Ch'eng Hsi was born in Hopei Province. He took his first degree at Yenching University in Peking, and later his mastership at Cambridge.

He has travelled much, starting as a Research Assistant in the Academia Sinica in Taipeh and then teaching in the Universities of Hong Kong, Cambridge, London and Malaya. He is now an Associate Professor of Chinese of the University of Iowa, where he has recently been lecturing on poetry and drama.

He writes tz'u and plays, and we remember with delight his production of a Chinese K'un-ch'ü opera, with a foreign student cast, at the School of Oriental and African Studies in London. He is also a keen musician and singer, and has a strong sense of humour.

The tz'u chosen here is one of a collection published by him under the title *Yen Shan Tz'u* ('Lyrics from the Yen Mountains').

臨江仙

翻破陣雲征大地奮威狂舞塵

沙怒侵江海捲龍蛇掀波振浪

倏忽返天涯浩氣欲摧山嶽

動危峯矗立堪嗟長林日暮響

悲笳無邊落葉飄閃逐寒鴉

程曦錄舊作

60

P'u – Lin Chiang Hsien
(To the tune-title 'The Immortal by the River')

TYPHOON

Smashing the clouds' array it hurtles at earth;
Makes dust and sand dance madly in its power;
Harries seas and rivers, rolling
            dragons and serpents as it rages by!
Shearing combers, churning billows,
It suddenly passes over the edge of the sky.

If such prodigious force can shatter mountains
One lonely peak left standing merits praise!
As twilight touches the straggling wood
            a melancholy tune on a reed-pipe flows;
And leaves descending all around
In the cold, flutter and feint in the path of crows.

SHIH
T'ang Dynasty

琵琶行　　白居易

元和十年，余左遷九江郡司馬。明年秋，送客湓浦口。聞舟中夜彈琵琶者，聽其音，錚錚然，有京都聲。問其人，本長安倡女，嘗學琵琶於穆曹二善才。年長色衰，委身為賈人婦。遂命酒，使快彈數曲。曲罷憫然，自敘少小時歡樂事

PO CHÜ I

P'i P'a Hsing

THE SONG OF A GUITAR

* Translation of calligraphy facing this page appears on p. 207
and in Appendix, pp. 257–8

，今漂淪憔悴，徙於江湖間。余出官二
年，恬然自安，感斯人言，是夕覺有遷
謫意，因為長歌以贈之，凡六百一十二
言，命曰琵琶行。

潯陽江頭夜送客，楓葉荻花秋瑟瑟。主人下馬
客在船，舉酒欲飲無管絃；醉不成歡慘將別，
別時茫茫江浸月。忽聞水上琵琶聲，主人忘歸

'In the tenth year of Yüan Ho I was down-graded to take up the post of an assistant in the Prefecture of Kiukiang. In the following autumn I was seeing off a visitor at the mouth of the P'en-p'u River when, about midnight, I heard someone playing a guitar in a boat . . .'*

I was seeing a friend off at night on the river bank at Hsün-yang
With its maple leaves and plumed reeds in the autumn wind
    astir.
Dismounting to play the host I found my friend on board
    already.
We raised our glasses of wine to drink. We had no music there

And drinking failed to cheer us, too unhappy at thought of
    parting.
The hour of parting came: the brimming river drenched the
    moon.
Suddenly over the flood we heard the sound of a guitar:
The host forgot his journey back, the guest his journey on.

* The translation of the full Preface will be found in Appendix I, Notes
on Poems, p. 257–8.

客不發。尋聲闇問彈者誰？琵琶聲停欲語遲。

移船相近邀相見，添酒回燈重開宴。千呼萬喚

始出來，猶抱琵琶半遮面。轉軸撥絃三兩聲，

未成曲調先有情。絃絃掩抑聲聲思，似訴平生

不得志。低眉信手續續彈，說盡心中無限事。

輕攏慢撚抹復挑，初為霓裳後六么。大絃嘈嘈

如急雨，小絃切切如私語；嘈嘈切切錯雜彈，

We traced the sound and called in the dark to find out who was
  playing.
The music stopped; whoever wished to speak appeared unsure.
We moved our boat up closer so that each could see the other:
Wine was poured, the lamps re-lit, the dishes served once more.

We called again and again before she ventured out at last
Still carrying her guitar and with her face half hidden away.
She turned the pegs and plucking at the strings two or three
  times
Revealed before she played the depth of feeling in her play.

She sounded each string low and every note expressed a thought,
Telling its tale of longing unfulfilled her whole life through.
With bended brow and practised hand she settled down to
  playing,
Pouring out her heart in bursts she set no limit to.

Her fingers combed the strings, caressed and swept and plucked
  again:
The Rainbow Skirt led off and then the Lu Yao's beat was
  heard.
Loudly spoke the heavy strings cascading down like rain,
The light in gentlest murmurs, each a secret whispered word;

大珠小珠落玉盤。間關鶯語花底滑，幽咽流泉水下灘。水泉冷澀絃凝絕，凝絕不通聲暫歇。別有幽情暗恨生，此時無聲勝有聲。銀瓶乍破水漿迸，鐵騎突出刀槍鳴，曲終收撥當心畫，四絃一聲如裂帛。東船西舫悄無言，惟見江心秋月白。沈吟放撥插絃中，整頓衣裳起歛容。自言本是京城女，家在蝦蟆陵下住。十三學得

Loudly, softly, mingling all together now and thrumming
Like large and lesser pearls let fall into a bowl of jade;
The song of birds, an oriole's liquid note among the flowers,
The quiet sob of spring water in some remote cascade.

Then, as though the spring had frozen, so the strings were
   stilled;
Frozen, stilled, without a sound one instant so they stayed
In muted grief that brought to life the secret depth of sorrow.
In that moment silence meant far more than had she played.

Suddenly a silver vase was shattered, scattering water;
Armoured horsemen thundered by with clashing spear and
   sword.
The tune was done; her plectrum swept the heart of her guitar;
To a sound like tearing silk the four strings played a single
   chord.
We spoke no word; spell-bound there on either side of the boat
We watched on the river's depths the dazzle of autumn moon-
   light float.

Deeply disturbed she slipped the plectrum back between the
   strings
And smoothing down her dress stood up, her face composed
   and still.
She began to speak, 'As a girl I was brought up in the capital;
My childhood home was at the foot of the Hsia-mo hill.
By the age of thirteen I had learned to play the guitar
And my name was ranked in the music school among the best
   of my year.

琵琶成，名屬教坊第一部；曲罷常教善才服，

妝成每被秋娘妒。五陵年少爭纏頭，一曲紅綃

不知數。鈿頭銀篦擊節碎，血色羅裙翻酒污。

今年歡笑復明年，秋月春風等閒度。弟走從軍

阿姨死，暮去朝來顏色故，門前冷落車馬稀，

老大嫁作商人婦！商人重利輕別離，前月浮梁

買茶去，去來江口守空船，繞船明月江水寒。

'As for my singing, eminent masters of music used to acclaim
    me;
My looks aroused the jealousy even of beauties like Ch'iu
    Niang.
The capital's gallants competed to give me the most song-
    money.
I could not count the rosy silks I earned for just one song!

'Silver hairpins and combs lay broken and crushed as I struck
    the measure,
Skirts of silk were stained blood-red in wine-spilt revelry;
This year's pleasure and laughter furnished next year's laughter
    and pleasure;
Unnoticed, autumn moons and winds of spring went slowly by.

'Then my younger brother joined the army and my aunt died.
Mornings followed evenings and my looks began to fade.
Horse or carriage seldom stirred the quiet of our gateway.
Older, seeking marriage, I became a merchant's bride.

'Profit counts for much in trading, separation little:
He went away last month to Fou-liang to buy some tea,
Leaving me here to guard an empty boat at the river's mouth
Where the moon glitters on the cold waters for ever surrounding
    me.
In the depths of night there suddenly comes a dream of my
    younger days
And I cry aloud and wake to find the tears furrow my face.'

夜深忽夢少年事，夢啼妝淚紅闌干！我聞琵琶

已嘆息，又聞此語重唧唧！同是天涯淪落人，

相逢何必曾相識！我從去年辭帝京，謫居臥病

潯陽城；潯陽地僻無音樂，終歲不聞絲竹聲。

住近湓城地低濕，黃蘆苦竹繞宅生，其間旦暮

聞何物？杜鵑啼血猿哀鳴，春江花朝秋月夜，

往往取酒還獨傾，豈無山歌與村笛，嘔啞嘲哳

I had sighed already to the sounds of her guitar
And now that I had heard her story I felt sadder still.
'Strangers from far away yet linked together in misfortune,
We meet – what need to have met before who share each other's
    ill?

'A year ago I said goodbye to the Imperial City,
Posted – banished rather – to a sick-bed in Hsün-yang;
Hsün-yang, so isolated and devoid of any music,
I haven't heard the sound of string or wood the whole year long.

'I live on damp low-lying ground close by P'en-p'u city;
Where yellowing reeds and sour bamboos surround the house;
And what is there to listen to from morning until evening
But the night-bird's cry to chill the blood and the apes' desolate
    cries!

'On the river in spring, in the season of flowers, by the autumn
    moon at night
Time and again I have brought out wine only to drink it alone.
Of course there are the mountain songs they play on a rustic
    flute
But it's punishment to listen to each painful squeak and groan.

難為聽。今夜聞君琵琶語，如聽仙樂耳暫明。

莫辭更坐彈一曲，為君翻作琵琶行。感我此言

良久立，卻坐促絃絃轉急，淒淒不似向前聲，

滿座重聞皆掩泣。座中泣下誰最多？江州司馬

青衫濕！

'This evening when I heard you giving speech to your guitar
Each moment sounds of fairy music seemed to bless my ear.
Don't go; sit down again and play another tune for us,
And I shall write a verse for you, the Song of a Guitar!'

Moved by what I said she stood there motionless awhile;
Then, seated, plucked and urged the strings into a frantic strain,
Anxious, afflicted, quite unlike the music heard before;
Yet every listener felt the need to hide his tears again.
Among those weeping listeners there, who was worst beset?
This official from Chiang-chou with sleeve darkened and wet!

天生麗質難自棄一朝選在君王側
回眸一笑百媚生六宮粉黛無顏色
節白居易 長恨歌

PO CHÜ I

Ch'ang Hên Ko

THE SONG OF ENDLESS SORROW

長恨歌　　　白居易

漢皇重色思傾國，御宇多年求不得。楊家有女
初長成，養在深閨人未識。天生麗質難自棄，
一朝選在君王側。回頭一笑百媚生，六宮粉黛
無顏色。春寒賜浴華清池，溫泉水滑洗凝脂；
侍兒扶起嬌無力，始是新承恩澤時。雲鬢花顏
金步搖，芙蓉帳暖度春宵；春宵苦短日高起，

Consumed by hunger for beauty that wrecks a kingdom, China's
    Lord
After reigning many years was searching for it still;
While a girl of the family of Yang, not yet fully grown,
Was brought up deep in the women's quarters unremarked by
    all.

But no one of such natural beauty could for long stay hidden
And one day she was chosen to enjoy the Emperor's favour.
A side-long glance, a single smile, so many charms were born
That the painted ladies of the Six Palaces lost their colour.

Invited to bathe in the cool of spring in the Hua-ch'ing pool
Its warming flow caressed and smoothed her alabaster skin.
A maid helping that languorous body to rise in all its beauty
Marked the occasion for the Emperor's favours to begin.

With cloud-dressed hair, rose-petal cheeks, she walked, gold
    trinkets swaying;
Behind hibiscus-dyed bed-curtains warm spring nights were
    passed –
Spring nights that seemed too harshly short before the sun rose
    high.
From this time on the Emperor's early morning audience ceased.

從此君王不早朝。承歡侍宴無閒暇，春從春游

夜專夜。後宮佳麗三千人，三千寵愛在一身。

金屋妝成嬌侍夜，玉樓宴罷醉和春。姊妹弟兄

皆列土，可憐光彩生門戶，遂令天下父母心，

不重生男重生女。驪宮高處入青雲，仙樂風飄

處處聞，緩歌謾舞凝絲竹，盡日君王看不足。

漁陽鼙鼓動地來，驚破霓裳羽衣曲。九重城闕

Taking his favours, attendant at feasts, her daily life was filled;
In spring, on spring excursions; nightly, night's companion.
Inside the Women's Palaces there were three thousand beauties:
With her three thousand favourites were embodied into one.
She adorned herself in her Golden Room to await on him at
    night;
The feasting over in the Jade Tower, what ecstasy of delight!

Her brothers and sisters were all awarded titles and estates
Raising the family to such an enviable splendour
That fathers and mothers everywhere found it in their hearts
To look upon a son as less important than a daughter!

High above where the Li Palace enters the cloudy blue
On winds from every quarter whirling fairy music rang,
Of slow song and stately dance with string and wood-wind
    playing.
The Emperor could not have enough and listened all day long.
Until, earth-shaking, out of Yü-yang sounded drums of war
And the 'Rainbow Skirt and Feather Jacket' song was stilled in
    fear.

煙塵生，千乘萬騎西南行。翠華搖搖行復止，

西出都門百餘里，六軍不發無奈何，宛轉蛾眉

馬前死！花鈿委地無人收，翠翹金雀玉搔頭。

君王掩面救不得，回看血淚相和流。黃埃散漫

風蕭索，雲棧縈紆登劍閣，峨嵋山下少人行，

旌旗無光日色薄。蜀江水碧蜀山青，聖主朝朝

暮暮情。行宮見月傷心色，夜雨聞鈴腸斷聲。

Smoke and dust obscure the Imperial City's towers and gates;
South-westwards now ten thousand horse, a thousand chariots
     file;
The Emperor's kingfisher banner flutters and waves, leads on –
     then stops
West of the capital's gates, a distance of over a hundred mile.
The Six Armies refuse to advance; trapped inexorably
He has no choice; to placate the soldiers moth-browed beauty
     must die.

Filagree hair-pins fall to the ground, nobody picks them up;
Kingfisher head-dress, golden bird, comb and hair-pin of jade.
The Sovereign hides his face, there is nothing he can do to save
     her;
Then turns to look where, mingled now, her blood, his tears had
     flowed.

Yellow dust is everywhere, a mournful wind is sighing.
Climbing Chien-ko the mountain pathways turn and twist.
Not many people choose to travel under O-mei Shan.
Banners fail to dazzle where the sunlight thins in mist.

In Szechwan with its rivers icy-jade and mountains blue
Day by day and night by night the Emperor brooded apart.
To see the moon as he travelled in state re-opened memory's
     wounds,
And to hear the rain at night on the tinkling roof-bells tore his
     heart.

天旋地轉迴龍馭，到此躊躇不能去！馬嵬坡下
泥土中，不見玉顏空死處！君臣相顧盡霑衣，
東望都門信馬歸。歸來池苑皆依舊，太液芙蓉
未央柳，芙蓉如面柳如眉，對此如何不淚垂？
春風桃李花開日，秋雨梧桐葉落時，西宮南內
多秋草，落葉滿階紅不掃。梨園弟子白髮新，
椒房阿監青娥老！夕殿螢飛思悄然，孤燈挑盡

The heavens revolved, the sun moved round; the Dragon train
    turned back,
But reaching that sad place he could not bring himself to pass.
There on the Ma-wei slope, the sunk and muddied earth among,
Her jade-smooth features were not found, only death's
    emptiness.
Rulers and ministers eyed each other, tear-wet coats on all,
Looked east, then gave their horses rein to the gates of the
    capital.

When he returned the lake and gardens were the same as ever;
Beside T'ai-yeh, hibiscus, and at Wei-yang, willow.
Hibiscus conjured up her face, the willow's curve her eye-brows;
Confronted by such visions how could tears fail to flow?
Winds of spring come blowing, blossom of peach and plum
    awaken:
Rains of autumn fall, away the wu-t'ung leaves are shaken.

In the southern grounds of the West Palace the autumn grass is
    rank,
Fallen leaves have spread the steps with flame and lie unswept.
The actors of the Pear Garden have grown their first white
    hairs;
From the eunuchs of the Pepper Room the bloom of youth has
    dropped.

未成眠。遲遲鐘鼓初長夜，耿耿星河欲曙天。

鴛鴦瓦冷霜華重，翡翠衾寒誰與共？悠悠生死

別經年，魂魄不曾來入夢。臨邛道士鴻都客，

能以精誠致魂魄，為感君王輾轉思，遂教方士

殷勤覓。排雲馭氣奔如電，升天入地求之徧，

上窮碧落下黃泉，兩處茫茫皆不見。忽聞海上

有仙山，山在虛無縹緲間。樓閣玲瓏五雲起，

At evening fireflies dance in the chamber where he broods in
   silence;
The wick's pulled out in his single lamp yet sleep is not yet won;
Slowly bell and drum drag through the first long hours of night;
The twinkling glow of the Milky Way brightens before the
   dawn.

Tiles of Mandarin drake and duck through layers of hoar-frost
   sparkle,
Cold creeps under his kingfisher cock-and-hen quilt – who's
   with him to share it?
Far, far from each other, one living, one dead, a year since they
   parted –
Yet never since then to visit the world of his dreams had she
   ventured her spirit.

A Taoist priest from Lin-ch'iung who visited the city
Could make his way by faith to regions where the immortals are.
Watching the Emperor brooding over his obsession
They begged the priest to search with the utmost diligence for
   her.

Flying up to the sky he rode its airy ways like lightning,
Climbed to heaven, sank into earth, enquiring everywhere.
From the bounds of the Blue Sublime above to the Yellow
   Springs below
He made his search without success through each stupendous
   sphere.

By chance he heard of a mountain of Immortals in the seas,
An insubstantial mountain set in visionary space;
Elegant tall pavilions with the Five Clouds rising round them,
And in them many immortals full of beauty and of grace,
And one immortal called T'ai-chen dwelling among them there
With snow-white skin, a flower-like face – he thought, could
   this be her?

其中綽約多仙子。中有一人字太真，雪膚花貌

參差是。金闕西廂叩玉扃，轉教小玉報雙成。

聞道漢家天子使，九華帳裏夢魂驚。攬衣推枕

起徘徊，珠箔銀屏迤邐開。雲鬢半偏新睡覺，

花冠不整下堂來。風吹仙袂飄飄舉，猶似霓裳

羽衣舞。玉容寂寞淚闌干，梨花一枝春帶雨。

含情凝睇謝君王：一別音容兩渺茫！昭陽殿裏

At the western court of the Gold Palace he knocked on the jade
    door,
Telling Hsiao-yü to send a message on to Shuang-ch'eng.
When the lady heard of an envoy from the Son of Heaven
Her spirit started from the nine-flowered silks she dreamed
    among.

Snatching at clothes she pulled away the pillows and rose
    unsure;
Pushed aside and swept through beaded curtain and silver
    screen.
Newly aroused from sleep, with clouds of hair dressed half awry
And garland hanging loosely, to the terrace she sped on.

With a breeze blowing diaphanous sleeves to fill and float
    behind her
As though she was dancing the 'Rainbow Skirt and Feather
    Jacket' there.
Tears had streaked their tracery over that sad and beautiful face
As the rain in spring-time streaks the bough that blossoms on
    the pear.

Hiding emotion under a front of ice she thanked the Emperor –
'Once we were parted, the other's voice and features began to
    fade;
Kindness and love I knew in the Chao-yang Palace were lost to
    me;
Days and months in the Palace of the Immortals lengthened
    instead.

恩愛絕，蓬萊宮中日月長。回頭下望人寰處，不見長安見塵霧。惟將舊物表深情，鈿合金釵寄將去，釵留一股合一扇，釵擘黃金合分鈿；但教心似金鈿堅，天上人間會相見！臨別殷勤重寄詞，詞中有誓兩心知，七月七日長生殿，夜半無人私語時：在天願作比翼鳥，在地願為連理枝。天長地久有時盡，此恨綿綿無絕期！

'Now when I turn my head to look down at the world of men
I cannot see Ch'ang-an but only dust and cloud below.
To show my depth of feeling I have chosen a few old trinkets –
A golden filagree box and hair-pin – take them with you and go!

'I have kept a part of the hair-pin and part of the lid of the box;
These broken bits from the hairpin and the filagree box I split
Are tokens to persuade our hearts to stay as true as gold,
Until in heaven above or in the world of men we meet.'

Earnestly, just before the envoy left, she added a message;
Its words revealed an oath two loving hearts alone could know.
On the seventh day of the seventh month in the Ch'ang-sheng
    Palace,
At midnight, no one else being present, this had been their vow –
'In heaven, as birds embraced that fly on one another's wings;
On earth, as branches interlaced, each branch so twines and
    clings!'

The heavens abide, earth endures; one day both will end.
This sorrow is an endless thread unwinding endlessly.

APPENDIX I

Notes on Poems

WEI YING WU

1 P'u – Tiao Hsiao

Stanza I, line 1 The higher grass-lands to the north and west of China were the breeding grounds of a stocky, tough type of horse, descended from the tarpan (Equus przewalskii)* which provided the Mongols and Tartars with their main attacking force – mounted archers.

Stanza I, line 3 'Yen-chih-shan'. 'Yen-chih-shan' is the name of a range of hills in the far north-west and is almost certainly the Chinese transliteration of a Mongol or Tartar place-name. The Chinese characters used differ in anthologies and do not lend themselves to translation. One form, as pronounced in Chinese, could have been understood to mean 'The Hill of Paint and Powder' and it was said that when, on one occasion, the Chinese captured Yen-chih-shan from the 'barbarians' a song was composed for them

> We've lost our Yen-chih-shan,
> So our womenfolk will be without make-up

Stanza II, line 5 'The river south'. The Chinese refers to Chiang-nan (literally 'river south', i.e. south of the Yangtze River) which was the name of the province now roughly corresponding with the provinces of Kiangsu, Anhwei, Chekiang, Fukien, Kiangsi, and Hunan.

Stanza II, line 8 'For us the Milky Way, all other roads are cut'. The distance between the man on the frontier in the north and his girl in the south would preclude any visit. In mentioning the Milky Way as providing the only link in its arc over the sky the poet would also undoubtedly have had in mind the legend of the Weaver-girl and the Herd-boy (see note on Ch'in Kuan's poem (No. 26, p. 91).

* For details on the horses of these times see Professor Schafer's *The Golden Peaches of Samarkand*, pp. 58–70.

CHANG CHIH HO

2 P'u – Yü Fu

Stanza I, line 1 'Herons', the white birds found in the rice-fields and near water, commonly called egrets or paddy-birds and more correctly Buff-backed Herons (Ardeola ibis).

Stanza I, line 2 'Where peach trees blossom' – could also be translated 'At peach-blossom time'.

Stanza V, line 3 'Then armed with fishing reels'. These reels, fixed like ours today at the foot of the rod (i.e. closest to the hand), are well illustrated by Wu Chên (A.D. 1280–1354), a Yüan dynasty artist, on a scroll in the Freer Gallery, Washington D.C. Professor Needham (*Science and Civilisation in China*, Vol. IV: 2, p. 100) draws attention to what may be an early reference to such a fishing-reel in the story of Tou Tzu-ming, in a text dated third or fourth century A.D., i.e. some 400 years before Chang Chih-ho wrote the poem translated here. As in this poem the reference is to a 'tiao ch'ê' (fishing wheel) which must surely refer to a reel.

PO CHÜ I

3 P'u – Lang T'ao Sha

Stanza III, line 1 Ch'ing-ts'ao Lake (lit. Green Grass Lake) was a common name and there would be many of them.

Stanza III, line 2 The apricot (lit. yellow plum) rain was a steady downpour, associated with their ripening.

Stanza V, line 2 reads literally in the Chinese 'On the top of a mountain, changed to stone' and this would at first sight lead one to think Po Chü-i was referring to the well-known legend of the faithful wife who looked out from a hilltop for her absent husband and waited for him so long that she eventually turned to stone. (See Ho Chu's use of this legend; Poem 28, p. 99, and Notes on Poems, p. 245.) But as is evident from what follows the poet was referring to the appearance of fossils as a result of the geological upheavals in the configuration of the earth, that is to say the rising of the sea-bottom to become dry land; as he says in Stanza II, line 4: 'Finally the mighty seas are turned to farming land' (lit. 'mulberry orchards', but the expression came to signify more generally land capable of being farmed).

Dr Needham in his monumental work (*Science and Civilisation in China*, Vol. III, p. 598 et seq.) quotes from an essay written by Yen Chên-ch'ing in about A.D. 770: 'Even in stones and rocks on lofty heights there are shells of oysters and clams to be seen. Some think that they were transformed from the groves and fields once under the water.' He goes on to point out that Yen was himself quoting from earlier sources written sometime between the second and sixth centuries (A.D.).

Pu Chü-i not only drew his inspiration from the earlier essays referred to, but freely borrowed from them, e.g. Stanza II, line 4 quoted above and Stanza V, line 1 'the dust will have its day and fly where ocean had its bed' are direct quotations.

WEI CHUANG

4 P'u – P'u Sa Man

Stanza I, verse 2, line 1 'guitar' – the p'i p'a, in fact a lute.
Stanza II, line 1 'Chiang-nan' – see Note on Poem I, Stanza II, line 5.
Stanza III, lines 1–2 Loyang was the second capital city (to Ch'ang-an) in the T'ang dynasty. Invasion from the north and rebellion had had the usual effect of a migration of the educated class further south.

FÊNG YEN SSU

6 P'u – Yeh Chin Mên

The setting of the poem, much admired by Chinese, would appear to be in a well-appointed garden with ornamental water and painted railings. The customary economy of language leaves a great deal to the imagination of the reader, but it may well be that the wrinkling of the pond alludes to a woman's furrowed brow, and the mandarin ducks (signifying conjugal fidelity) and crumpling of flowers to the anxiety which so distracts her. But Fêng Yên-ssu's Monarch, a poet in his own right, obviously did not hold to the idea of trying to read too much into every line, for he is said to have remarked when they were discussing the poem together, 'What has "The wind suddenly rises and blows the whole pond of spring water into wrinkles" got to do with it?'
Verse 2, line 1 The Chinese reads literally, character by character, 'Fighting duck(s) railing(s) alone lean'. The Chinese certainly watched duck-fighting in the fourth century A.D. for there is a story that Lu Hsün, a minister of one of the ruling family (Sun Lü) of the Wu Kingdom, told his master that he

would be better employed reading the classics than enjoying this form of sport. But there is no question of the birds actually fighting here, for the scene has been set with the faithful pair of mandarin ducks. The interpretation given to these first two characters therefore is likely to be a description of the railings, either in the form of a painted frieze or of a style associated with a fighting main. In the latter case, for instance, the pond where ducks used to fight might have benches, equipped with backs but with the seats facing outwards from the pond. Onlookers, on the occasion of 'a main', would turn sideways and lean (p'ien i) over the back of the bench to watch the contest.

Verse 2, line 4 The magpie's call was taken to be a happy omen.

FÊNG YEN SSU

7 P'u – Tsui Hua Chien

Verse 2, line 2 'Chin-ling' – the old name for the present Nanking.

FÊNG YEN SSU

8 P'u – Ch'iao T'a Chih

Verse 1, line 4 'at Ch'ing-ming Eve'. Ch'ing-ming was the spring festival when the Chinese paid their respects at the family graves. The chances were good therefore that the young man in this case, who had been away for some time, might reappear in his native town for this gathering.

P'AN LANG

9 P'u – Chiu Ch'üan Tzu

Stanza I, verse 2, line 2 'White birds' – see Notes on Poems, Chang Chih Ho, No. 2, p. 236.
Stanza II 'Tidal bore' and 'tidal riders' – see Biographical Note on P'an Lang, p. 41.

LIN PU

10 P'u – Ch'ang Hsiang Ssu

Verse 1, lines 1–2 Wu-shan (Wu hill) and Yüeh-shan (Yüeh hill): and

Verse 2, line 4 'Already the tide runs deep in the estuary' – see Biographical Note on Lin Pu, p. 47.

CHANG HSIEN

11 P'u – Kêng Lou Tzu

Verse 1, line 1 Red is the colour for happiness.

CHANG HSIEN

12 P'u – Ch'ing Mên Yin

Verse 1, line 3 'Ch'ing-ming' – see Notes on Poems, Poem No. 8, p. 238.
Verse 2, line 2 'the many doors', that is the many doorways which led from one courtyard and set of buildings to the next, all of which would be closed at night. The women's quarters lay at the back of the complex of buildings and would be inaccessible to the ordinary visitor.

YEN SHU

13 P'u – Shan T'ing Liu

Verse 1, line 1 The old state of Ch'in roughly occupied the area now known as Shensi province.
Verse 1, line 5 Nien-nu – a popular singing-girl of the eighth century A.D.
Verse 2, line 6 'the difficult "Yang Ch'un" song'. In fact, this was an ancient song of Ch'u – of the Spring and Autumn era – and neither the singing-girl, nor even the scholars of the time, are likely to have been acquainted with its many details.

SU SHIH

15 P'u – Shao Nien Yu (written when he was thirty-nine years old)

Verse 1, line 2 The 'Yü-hang Gate' was one of the main gates, in the extreme north-west corner, of the city of Hangchow. Yü-hang – so called after the Emperor Yü (see Poem No. 40, p. 141) – was one of the ancient names for the city, and now is the name of a village lying a few miles to the north.
Verse 2, line 2 'Window-gauze'. Windows were usually of paper

pasted over the wooden lattice-work, but in an inner courtyard of a richer house they might be of thin silk or gauze.

Verse 2, line 3 'Chang-O' is a figure in Chinese mythology. She stole the Pill of Immortality from her husband, Shên I, who had hidden it in the rafters of his house. Swallowing it she was wafted up to the moon.

SU SHIH

16   P'u – Jui Chê Ku

Verse 1, line 2 'Red boats' were the boats of officials.
Verse 1, line 4 'a pair of ducks' – Su Shih is probably poking fun at the two Magistrates waiting for their Prefect.
Verse 2, line 4 Compare this line with his poem to Chao Tuan-yen (see 'The Gay Genius' by Lin Yü T'ang, pp. 131–2):

Why not dismiss your retinue
And borrow a couch from the monk
Read the poems I inscribed on the rocks,
And let the cool mountain air soothe your troubled soul?

SU SHIH

17   P'u – Ch'in Yüan Ch'un

This is one of the poems which Su Shih wrote to his brother Tzu-yu (another, his 'Ode to the August Moon' will be found in our *Collection of Chinese Lyrics*). One of the most charming traits in Su Shih's character is the deep affection and loyalty he had for this younger brother; they were obviously devoted to one another.

Su Shih prefaces this poem with a note that he wrote it on his way from Hangchow to Michow, where he was taking up the post of Chief Magistrate. He would be a good deal closer to Tzu-yu at Michow, though it cannot have been anything like as pleasant a place to live in as Hangchow.

Line 15 'Like the Lu brothers'. The Lu's were two brothers of a well-known family who served in the Wu kingdom at the time of the Three Kingdoms (A.D. 222–277).
Line 18 'Yao or Shun'. These were two legendary Kings who are said to have ruled over the country in about 2200 B.C. and were held to be models of wisdom and kingly virtue.

240

SU SHIH

18 P'u – Chiang Ch'êng Tzu.

'Ten years ago . . .' This poem was written in 1075 – when Su
Shih was thirty-nine years old – ten years after his first wife's
death; she was only twenty-six when she died, leaving Su Shih
with one son. As was the strict custom Su Shih had resigned his
post at the capital and taken both his wife's and his father's
coffins back to his home town, Meishan, in Szechuan province.
There, it is said, he planted pine trees by the graves on the hill.

Commentators point to this poem as evidence that Su Shih
was not such an unfeeling character as his critics were apt to
make him out to be.

SU SHIH

19 P'u – Chiang Ch'êng Tzu

Verse 1, line 8 'that old-time warrior'. Su Shih here compares
himself to the famous warring sovereign of the Three Kingdoms
period, Sun Ch'üan.
Verse 2, lines 4/5 These lines refer to an incident in the Han
Dynasty when an official named Wei was banished by the
Emperor. Another official, Fêng T'ang, stood up for Wei and
secured the Emperor's agreement to reinstate him.
Verse 2, line 8 A literal translation of the Chinese is 'Shoot the
Heaven-(ly) Wolf', and Su Shih is quoting from a line in the
Ch'u Tz'u – 'I aim my long arrow and shoot the Wolf of
Heaven', where the Wolf of Heaven is a star (see *Ch'u Tz'u* by
David Hawkes, O.U.P. 1959, p. 42). Su Shih 'keeping watch
north-westwards' is referring to the troubles with the barbarian
tribes on the Tibetan–Mongolian frontier.

SU SHIH

20 P'u – Wan Ch'i Sha. Thanksgiving for Rain.

Stanza I, line 6 Grammatically this line should be translated
'When I return I will tell the girls picking mulberries', but it
would seem to be more logical – not always a reliable guide – to
adopt our rendering.
Stanza III, line 3 The last three characters of this line literally
meaning 'reel(ing) silk thread girl(s)' can also be applied to
crickets, from the continuous noise they make. They could be

translated here in either sense, but the poet does in fact seem to be occupied with the operations in silk-making.

SU SHIH

21 P'u – Wan Ch'i Sha

A Chinese commentator has suggested that this poem would read more logically in a different order, first taking lines 1 and 2 (about the harvest), then lines 3 and 6 (about garden flowers) and finally lines 4 and 5 (describing the general scene). But we have preserved Su Shih's original order bringing out, in contradiction to the usual melancholy parting scenes so popular with the poets of that time, Nature's vigour – in bumper harvest, in the beauty of flowers, and in giving happiness to old and young.
Verse 1, line 1 The opening two characters which today read 'ashamed' have completely changed their meaning in the last 800 years. Su Shih meant that such a harvest had seldom been seen – it was a lucky chance.
Verse 2, line 2 We have assumed that the first character in this line should be read as 'lan' (with the 'hand' radical) meaning 'to block'.
Verse 2, line 3 The flower (Chin-hsün-lung) is interpreted to be the same as Jui-hsiang-hua, which is the scented daphne (Daphne odora), one of the most beautifully scented of all bushes which has been brought to this country from China by the earlier plant-hunters, and one colloquially known to the Chinese as the 'thousand-mile-scent' flower.

SU SHIH

22 P'u – Ting Fêng P'o

Verse 1, line 2 'boom and bellow' in the rain. The Abbé Huc in the mid-nineteenth century in China (*The Chinese Empire* by M. Huc, Longmans, Brown Green and Longmans, 1855), travelling in just such weather, wrote, 'the palanquin-bearers appeared quite delighted when they felt the rain running down their backs . . . they burst into peals of laughter; they sang with all their might and main. . . .'; this translator has had similar experiences travelling in the interior.
Verse 2, lines 4–6 Su Shih having emerged from a rain storm into sunshine is comparing his own happy situation (at Tung-

242

p'o) with the unpredictable nature of life in the capital and its unfair bias and capriciousness.

SU SHIH

23 P'u – Wan Ch'i Sha

Verse 2, line 2 'river . . . flowing towards the west'. As all the great rivers of China flowed east from the central Asian highlands to the sea, this was frequently quoted as a changeless phenomenon of nature. But Su Shih quotes a case to show that this particular theory, used to illustrate the irreversible passing of time, need not be taken too seriously.
Verse 2, line 3 Su Shih is referring to Po Chü-i's poem:
Who says that a traveller cannot understand a song
As he listens to the cock crow at dawn?
The yellow cock hastens the dawn and crows before light;
The sun hastens the passing of time as darkness falls.
A red sash is not even securely tied round the waist
Before youth sees in the mirror it is losing the race against time.

SU SHIH

24 P'u – Lin Chiang Hsien

Verse 1, line 1 'Tung-p'o' was the plot of land (lit. Eastern Slope) which he cultivated in the hills. From his house he looked down on to the Yangtze. He had been banished to this district for his outspoken views on Government affairs, and he was not allowed to move far from it, though he could visit friends and even cross the river to a temple on the other side. He was about forty-six years old when he wrote this.
Verse 1, line 2 'Third Watch' – 11 p.m. to 1 a.m.

SU SHIH

25 P'u – Tieh Lien Hua

Verse 2 The background of this verse is the cloistered nature of a Chinese house, and particularly of its female occupants. High walls protected them from the street both in their apartments and their courtyard playground, and many doors (see Chang Hsien, Poem No. 12, p. 55) lay between them and the outside world.

243

CH'IN KUAN

27 P'u – Wang Hai Ch'ao

Ch'in Kuan wrote this poem at Loyang, one of the Sung capital cities, on his return after retiring from Government life.

Verse 1, line 3 The east wind brought spring with it.

Verse 1, line 5 'Bronze Camel Street' so named because there was a bronze statue of a camel at the end of the main street of the city.

Verse 1, line 6 'The sanded road'. Senior Government officials were entitled to have sand spread on the street in front of their houses; the poet therefore was strolling in the fashionable residential district.

HO CHU

28 P'u – Shêng Ch'a Tzu

This verse perhaps gives one a good example of the conciseness of the literary Chinese and, due to the absence of articles, pronouns, genders, inflexions, and punctuation, the wide variety of interpretation open to the reader. The poem consists of eight lines, each of five characters, and translated literally, character by character, would read:

West   creek   sea   hawk   boat
Straight   cross over   wide/grey   river   rain
Pair   oars   basic(ally)   without   feeling
Ya-   cha(croaking, like the cawing of crows)   like man('s)
      conversation
Scatter   gold   path   on   husband/young man
Change   stone   hill   top   wife
What   matter/thing   anxious about   you(r)/person('s) heart
Three   year   support   bed   girl

The literary allusions and one or two small points can be explained as follows:

Verse 1, line 1 'Sea hawk'. This could either mean a boat 'as swift as a hawk' or one with its bow fashioned or painted to look like a hawk.

Verse 2, line 1 The story behind this line is an old one about a certain Lu Ch'iu-hu who married a girl and then, after only five days, had to leave her with his parents to take up an official appointment elsewhere. He was away for five years and on

244

returning to his native village spotted a pretty girl in the mulberry orchards.

> Working hard is not as good as enjoying fine weather.
> Picking mulberry is not as good as meeting a high official.
> I have gold and would like to give it to you,

he said to her. To which she replied

> Picking mulberry I do with all my might.
> To look after my parents-in-law I spin, weave and provide food and clothing.
> I don't want your gold.

The official went on to his parents' house only to find that his wife was the girl in the mulberry-orchard. She was so ashamed of her husband's conduct that she drowned herself in the river. (Five years ago this translator saw the dramatized version of this in Peking. But, as is usual for the stage, the end is altered and the husband is left to grovel and apologize – and be forgiven.)

Verse 2, line 2 This allusion is to another legend about an official who was posted far away from his home, and where he was kept for many years during troubled times and great difficulties. His wife, who had borne him a son, refused to give up hope, and used to wait on a hill-top looking out for him so often that one day she turned to stone. (For the completely different meaning of these four characters in another context, 'Change stone hill top', see Po Chü-i's biographical note and Poem No. 3, pp. 15, 236)

Verse 2, line 4 In China a child is of 'one year' the day it is born, so the translation of the Chinese words 'three-year girl' is our 'two-year-old', just able to walk while hanging on to a bed for support.

The interpretation of these lines (see the biographical note on Ho Chu, p. 97) which appeals to us is that the mother, with a child hanging on to her for support, is in the boat, possibly ferrying it across herself, and that the poet imagines her having been left, if not deserted, by her husband, while she loyally carries on and ekes out a living. A different interpretation (made the more easy by reading the word 'chün' 'you/your' in the seventh line as normally being applied to a man) can place the husband, and not the wife, in the boat. The poet in this case asks him what is on his mind and receives the reply that it is his

润卿幽以弘，亭馭街訝俊探安備，高駈指曾眇仰，一飞長嚼壮妹敗，已三十功名塵与土，八乡黑語雲和月、等等窗白子少身張、悲切情康犯務末雪臣子北行時賊馭、長車論破賀蘭山、執壮志肌站的雲霧、由处谋洞飢匈奴窗络洪頭收拾舊雄山河、新天氣

嵩嵐

three-year-old child left with her mother for what may well be, or already has been, a long time.

CHOU PANG YEN

30 P'u – Shih Liu Tzu Ling

Line 2 white jade'. The Chinese literally refers to 'white jade cash'. Cash was their cheapest coin, made of metal with a square hole in the middle so that it could be strung together.

TS'AI SHÊN

31 P'u – Shih Liu Tzu Ling

Line 1 The word 'Heaven' has no religious significance here, but has much the same meaning, in this context, as we use when we say 'Old Man of the Moon'.
Line 2 'full moon' – literally written here as 'Round Toad'. This alludes to one version of a legend that Ch'ang O (see p. 240) having stolen the Pill of Immortality, flew to the moon and was changed into a toad.
Line 4 A further allusion to the moon is made here by referring to it as the 'cassia tree', as according to legend there are great numbers of these trees on it.

YÜEH FEI

P'u – Man Chiang Hung

The English translation of Yüeh Fei's calligraphy reproduced opposite is reprinted here from our first volume (Poem No. 56).

Brooding on it, blood boils, bristles prick with rage –
Hushed now, ceased, the rain-shower's hiss.
Looking out and up to heaven I roar with rage.
Passion fires my loyalties.
Dust, my thirty years of worth and fame;
Miles marched eight thousand; days, nights, parched or chill.
Who wastes himself and time;
Still young, lets hair grow white, spirit tame;
Long will grieve he did so ill.
Emperor Ching K'ang's shame
Shouts for vengeance still.

247

My hate for palace men
When shall I fulfil?
In one fierce chariot charge I'ld break
The gates of Ho Lan Shan and kill!
My ambition, hungry, is to eat the flesh of Huns;
Later, at my leisure, thirsty, drink the blood I spill!
Give me my chance again
To win back lake and mountain, stream and plain –
Then, I'll crave audience of the Emperor!

YÜEH FEI

33   P'u – Man Chiang Hung

Verse 1 The poet in this first verse refers to Pien-liang (now
K'ai-feng) the capital of the Sung Dynasty captured by the Chin
Tartars.

Verse 1, line 5 'Wan-sui-shan' (lit. 'The Hill of Ten Thousand
Years') was a park, complete with hill and flower gardens, which
the Emperor Hui-tsung (A.D. 1101–1125) commissioned to be
set up. (He was himself a painter and calligrapher in his own
right as well as being a patron of the arts.) The 'hill' would
probably have been an artificial one, with pavilions connected
by covered ways of painted pillars and beams winding round its
face, and cannot have been completed more than a few years
before the north, including its capitals, fell to the invading
Chin Tartars. In this translation we have assumed the fifth
character to be read as 'chu' meaning 'red' (and therefore here
taken as 'painted') rather than the form written in this particular
version meaning 'pearls'.

Verse 1, line 8 'armoured horsemen' – the Chin Tartars.

Verse 2, last line 'Riding his Yellow Crane' – see the bio-
graphical note for Yüeh Fei, p. 113.

CHU TUN JU

34   P'u – Hao Shih Chin

The poet has strung together five tz'u (each of two verses) of
which we translate four here. In the Chinese the words at the
end of each couplet in any one stanza – i.e. four words in a stanza
of eight lines – would rhyme.

Stanza II, lines 3–4 '. . . by the T'ung-t'ing lake' and 'by the
Ch'ien-t'ang river'. These two well-known pieces of water are in

fact some 400 miles apart, and though this would not be by any means an unheard of distance to cover the poet is simply conveying the idea of the fisherman's freedom of movement.
Line 8 'news about my friends' (lit. 'plum blossom news').

K'ANG YÜ CHIH

35 P'u – Ts'ai Sang Tzu (Ch'ou Nu Erh Ling)

Verse 1, line 1 Fêng I was the God of Waters and Rivers. Snow had a special fascination for the Chinese, particularly in the south (Yangtze Valley) where little fell. One poet, Mêng Hao-jan, used to 'look for plum blossom in the snow', and this is now interpreted broadly as 'seeking inspiration in the snow'.

FAN CH'ÊNG TA

36 P'u – I Ch'in O

Verse 2, line 1 'the water clock' or Clepsydra consisted of a series of water-containers, with the water dripping from one to the other to measure the time, on the same principle as an hourglass.
Verse 2, line 2 'Will the lamp-wick threads . . . spell out a message for me?' There was a superstition that as a lamp or candlewick burnt out and the ends frayed, some message – perhaps by the likeness to some Chinese character – might be apparent. The same fanciful notion was resorted to by love-sick girls when they looked for a message in the centre of a blossom.

LU YU

37 P'u – Pu Suan Tzu

Among Mao Tse-tung's published poems one will be found, referring specifically to this poem by Lu Yu, written also 'In Praise of Plum Blossom', to the same tune-pattern.

LU YU

38 P'u – Su Chung Ch'ing

Verse 1, line 1 'serving my country' (lit. 'seeking promotion to the nobility'). Lu Yu in using this expression is not seeking honours for himself but holding up the example of the famous Pan Ch'ao (A.D. 32–102), a military commander in the Later Han Dynasty. Pan Ch'ao's skill, courage and diplomacy dealing with the 'barbarian' tribes of the north-west enabled him to recover Chinese Turkestan and he is said at one time to have reached the shores of the Caspian. He died soon after returning to China, a worn-out man, and was posthumously raised to the nobility.

Verse 2, lines 5–6 'My heart far off in the T'ien Shan, my worn-out body in Ts'ang chou?' In his anxiety to make the most of his 'military' career he refers to the T'ien Shan mountains north of Chinese Turkestan (now the province of Sinkiang), a great deal further than he is ever likely to have gone! Ts'ang-chou was a place-name associated with retired scholars.

HSIN CH'I CHI

40   P'u – Shêng Ch'a Tzu

The poet in his preface makes it clear he is writing on the bank of the Yangtze River, opposite Golden (Hill) Isle. Something in the pavilion in which he sat or the sight of the river itself reminded him of Yü, the semi-legendary Emperor who is said to have founded the Hsia Dynasty in about 2000 B.C.

Dr Needham calls him 'Yü, the Great Engineer' (see *Science and Civilisation in China*, Vol. I, p. 87), for to him is attributed the monumental task of bringing the Yellow River under control, as a result of which the periodical floods were avoided and 'the people descended from the hills and dwelt in the plains' (see line 4 of this poem). Yü is said to have worked also on most of China's great waterways, and to have spent thirteen years continuously on this work, travelling, organizing and controlling great quantities of corvée labour. One legend about this unremitting toil and leadership (see line 2 of this poem) is that though he passed the door of his house on three occasions in the course of these years he never once took time off to see his family.

Verse 2 The first and second lines form 'a pair' and contrast the sun's sinking in the evening and rising in the morning with the river's constant flow in one direction only – eastward. This contrast lends point to the next couplet, with the last line accenting Yü's permanent achievement.

HSIN CH'I CHI

41   P'u – P'u Sa Man

Lines 1–2 The poet is reminded by the sight of the Ch'ing (Clear) River that this is where the Empress passed as she fled,

fifty years earlier, when the Tartars captured the Sung capital.
Line 7 Hsin Ch'i-chi closes this line with two characters (ch'ou yü) from the Ch'u Tz'u – Hsiang Fu Jen. (See David Hawkes' translation *Ch'u Tz'u – The Songs of the South*, O.U.P., 1959.)

> The Child of God, descending the northern bank
> Turns on me her eyes that are dark with longing.

HSIN CH'I CHI

43 P'u – Ch'ing P'ing Lê

Line 4 'tattered paper'. See Note on Su Shih – Shao Nien Yu (Poem No. 15, verse 2, line 2, p. 239).
Line 8 'Countless miles of river and mountain. . . .' The northern half of the country lost to the Tartars.

HSIN CH'I CHI

44 P'u – Hsi Chiang Yüeh

The poet in his preface writes that he was taking a stroll in the night.

HSIN CH'I CHI

45 P'u – Hsi Chiang Yüeh

A 'political' poem written in scarcely veiled language to describe how government policies were utterly at variance with accepted sound procedure, and the poet's refusal to consider any idea of getting involved.

HSIN CH'I CHI

47 P'u – Chê Ku T'ien

Verse 1, lines 1–2 The cultivation of silk must date back to very early times, certainly prior to the fifth century B.C. for, as Dr Needham points out in his *Science and Civilisation in China*, Vol. III, p. 501, the Yü Kung (Tribute of Yü) contains the following passage: 'The mulberry grounds were stocked with silkworms, and the people descended from the hills and dwelt in the plains.'

251

Lines 5–6 This tune-pattern prescribes that the fifth and sixth lines should form a 'pair', which is reflected in the English.

HSIN CH'I CHI

48   P'u – P'o Chên Tzu

Lines 3–5 The background here is of a series of parades and manœuvres on the frontier when the horses would be in good condition and ready for active service after the autumn rains. As a morale booster after the hot summer, training during the day was followed by feasting and music in the evening. The literal translation of line 3 is 'Eight hundred li [Chinese mile] divided amongst troops, roast'. It is obscure whether the 'eight hundred miles' refers to an area covered by the troops, or, as some say, to a type of oxen.

Line 6 'Liu Pei' was one of the great figures in the period of 'The Three Kingdoms' (about A.D. 221–277). He established himself as the ruler of Shu, the westernmost of the three rival powers.

HSIN CH'I CHI

49   P'u – Mu Lan Hua Man

Hsin Ch'i-chi in the first verse of this poem refers to the cosmological theories of his times, and in particular to the Hsüan Yeh Teaching (Infinite Empty Space) – see Dr Needham's *Science and Civilisation in China*, Vol. III, p. 219, et seq. – 'The sun, the moon and the company of the stars float (freely) in the empty space, moving or standing still . . . they are not rooted or tied together' says one writer (third century A.D.); and another in the thirteenth century wrote: 'How unreasonable it would be to suppose that besides the heaven and the earth which we can see there are no other heavens and no other earths!' (Compare Hsin Ch'i-chi in this poem, lines 4–8.)

Dr Needham continues in this same volume of his work (p. 222), 'But running through the centuries was an additional conception, that of the "hard wind" which helped the Chinese... to imagine that stars and planets could be borne along without being attached to anything' (see line 8 in this poem).

The second part of the poem, including the last two lines of the first verse, resorts to legends. One cosmological theory held that between two inverted bowls – the outer representing the heavens and the inner the earth – was a great trench of water,

252

and it was into this sea that the heavenly bodies plunged when they set. Hsin Ch'i-chi deals with the implications of these legends, and in particular with the immersion of the moon in the seas, when he refers to the moon by its various names, first the Goddess of the Moon, Ch'ang-O, and her dwelling places, the Jade Palace and Jasper Tower; then the Toad, according to one legend Ch'ang-O was changed into a Toad; and finally the Hare. (For further details of these legends see Werner's *Myths and Legends of China*, pp. 176–88.)

HSIN CH'I CHI

50   P'u – Shui Lung Yin

Verse 1, lines 1–12, Verse 2, lines 1–3 In his short preface to this poem Hsin Ch'i-chi mentions that he was passing by the Tower of the Twin Streams (Shuang Hsi Lou) which is in what is now known as Fukien Province. It was at this spot, so went the legend, that two magic swords lay in a deep pool.

A thousand years earlier, it was said, two men, Chang Hua and Lei Huan, had found a pair of swords of dazzling brightness. Chang Hua was murdered and his sword was lost. While Lei Huan was looking for it his own suddenly shot out of its scabbard and sank into a deep pool. Lei Huan, peering into the water, saw two dragons coiled in the depths.

The poet here expresses his view that the only weapon with which the Tartar invaders of China's northern territory can be cleared out is a 'sky-long' magic sword (Verse 1, lines 1–2) – See Sung Yü's 'Ta Yen Fu' for an early reference to such a sword. He then goes on to allude, almost certainly, to the Emperor's and his government's refusal to mount any counter-attack (Verse 2, lines 1–3) and to his own inability to remonstrate without endangering his life – that is to cope with 'wind's and thunder's rage, venom of fish and dragon', his scarcely veiled metaphor for the powers-that-be (Verse 1, lines 9–12).

Verse 2, line 4 'Yüan-lung' was the familiar name of one Ch'ên Têng who retired from worldly affairs and who did not even bother to rise from his bed when visitors called.

CHIANG K'UEI

P'u-An Hsiang
(*To the tune-title 'Secret Fragrance'*)

MOONLIGHT OF DAYS LONG OVERCOME

Chiu shih yüeh sê. Suan chi fan chao wo. Mei pien ch'ui ti.

Huan ch'i yü jên. Pu kuan ch'ing han yü p'an chai. Ho Hsün êrh

chin chien lao. Tu wang ch'io ch'un fêng tz'ǔ pi. Tan kuai tê, chu

wai su hua. Hsiang lêng ju yao hsi.

Chiang kuo. Chêng chi chi. T'an chi yü lu yao.

Yeh hsüeh ch'u chi. Ts'ui tsun i ch'i. Hung——o wu yen kêng hsiang i.

Ch'ang chi ts'eng hsi shou ch'u. Ch'ien shu ya Hsi — hu han pi.

Yu p'ien p'ien, ch'ui chin yeh. Chi shih chien tê.

CHIANG-K'UEI

P'u – An Hsiang

The English translation of this tz'u, for which the music is
printed opposite, is reprinted here from our first volume (Poem
No. 62).

Moonlight of days long overcome,
How many times it shone on me as I,
Piping my flute beside the plum,
Aroused your beauty with a serenade.
What cared I for the cold, or if you picked the spring blossom?
I sang then like Ho Hsün! – but now that I grow old
The lyric note is quite forgot, the voice of spring is dumb.
Yet still I marvel as from scattered flowers beyond the canes
Cool scented airs into my bedroom come.

On field and river
An utter stillness lies.
So long the road; and now the night-snows mass
All I can send as presents are my sighs.
This bowl of jade moves me to tears;
Mutely, this blossom conjures up shared shining memories.
But always I recall that walk when hand in hand
We saw the ice-green Western Lake clasped by a thousand trees.
Now every leaf is blown away.
When shall we see again what memory sees?

CHIANG K'UEI

51 P'u – Hsing Hua T'ien Ying

Chiang K'uei in his preface refers to Mien-k'ou, the present-day
Han-yang, and to Chin-ling, now known as Nanking. He
'looked north' to the country on the left bank of the lower
Yangtze River.
Verse 1, line 2 There was a ferry-point near Nanking called
after T'ao-yeh (Peach Leaf), a concubine of Wang Hsien Chih
(third century A.D.).
Verse 1, line 5 The poet here is quoting a couple of characters
from the Ch'u Tz'u (see David Hawkes' *Ch'u Tz'u – the Songs
of the South*, O.U.P., 1959, p. 38).

The cassia oars, the sweep of orchid
Churn the waters to foaming snow.

Verse 2, lines 1–2 The poet is probably reminding us of Liu Yü-hsi's description of Nanking; the tides with their daily flowing and ebbing see and know all man's problems.

Verse 2, line 3 This line is another reference to Ch'u Tz'u (see note on Verse 1, line 5 above).

CHIANG K'UEI

52 P'u – Tsui Yin Shang

Chiang K'uei explains in the preface to this tz'u that his patron Fan Ch'êng-ta (see p. 127), whom he greatly admired, had told him that this tune had got lost over the years. However, Chiang K'uei finds a lute-player who knows the tune and so having learnt it the poet composed these words to it.

Verse 2, line 1 'saddle of gold'. This phrase was a common one to denote the noble or rich owner of horse and trappings.

Verse 2, lines 2–3 Compare William Blake:

> Never seek to tell thy love,
> Love that never told shall be;
> For the gentle wind does move
> Silently, invisibly . . .

CHIANG K'UEI

54 P'u – Ch'ang T'ing Yüan Man

Verse 2, line 3 'the poet Wei' is Wei Kao (A.D. 746–806) of the T'ang Dynasty. The story about him is that on having to leave his concubine Yü-hsiao (Jade Flute) behind when he left to take up a distant post, he promised the girl that he would come back in not later than seven years time. When at the end of that period he had not appeared she committed suicide. Wei-Kao returned a year later.

Verse 2, line 7 'Knife from Ping'. Ping was the district where the best knives and swords were made.

SHIH TA TSU

55 P'u – Shuang Shuang Yen

Verse 1, line 4 The first two characters of this line ('tz'u ch'ih') are quoted from a much earlier poem in the ancient anthology, the Shih Ching, and refer to the 'uneven winging' of swallows, that is to the banking and tilting of wings as a swallow flies, particularly when near a wall or corner.

Verse 2, line 5 'red-beamed chamber'. The 'hung lou' usually referred to the women's quarters in a big house.

Verse 2, line 8 Swallows on migration were thought of as message-carriers in their passage from south to north in spring, and back again in the autumn.

Verse 2, line 9 'pencilled eye-brows'. The Chinese referred to a beautiful woman's eye-brows as 'moth's antennae' to match the latter's delicacy and sensitiveness.

LIU K'O CHUANG

56 P'u – Yü Lou Ch'un

Verse 2, line 1 'to get a verse embroidered on silk for you'. This is a literary allusion to the complicated piece of embroidery made by Su Hui, the wife of Tou T'ao (fourth century A.D.) who had been banished by his ruler to the north-west desert. His loyal wife occupied herself with the monumental work of embroidering 840 characters in a circular pattern, which she then dispatched to her husband.

WANG CH'ING HUI

57 P'u – Man Chiang Hung

Verse 2, lines 1–2 'Dragon and Tiger . . . Wind were gone'. This is a literary allusion to the might and majesty of the Imperial Government – 'The Dragon came out of the clouds; The Tiger came with the wind'.

Verse 2, line 9 'Ch'ang-O (see Su Shih – Shao Nien Yu – Note on Poem No. 15, verse 2, line 3, p. 240).

PO CHÜ I

P'i P'a Hsing: 'The Song of a Guitar', p. 205

Po Chü-i explains in a prefatory note to this poem how he came to write it. The note, in full, reads as follows:

'In the tenth year of Yüan Ho I was down-graded to take up the post of an assistant in the Prefecture of Kiukiang. In the following autumn I was seeing off a visitor at the mouth of the P'en-p'u River when, about midnight, I heard someone playing a guitar in a boat. Listening to the sound I recognized the string tones as those of the style played in the capital. On my asking the player, I gathered she had been a singing-girl in Ch'ang-an and had been taught to play the guitar by the two maestros Mu and Ts'ao. As she grew older and her beauty faded she had become a merchant's wife. Thereupon I ordered wine and at once asked her to play us some tunes; these finished, she sat sad and silent. She told us that after the happiness of her youth she had drifted to grief and distress, moving around from one place to another.

Since I had left my official post (in the capital) two years before, I had lived happy and content. But I was moved by what this girl had said that evening, and began to be conscious of my banishment. So I wrote a long poem (of 612 characters) as a dedication, calling it "The Song of a Guitar".'

Verse 1, line 1 'Hsün-yang', the place to which the poet had been banished in the district of Chiang-chou (the modern Kiukiang), was on the Yangtze River below Hankow.

Verse 4, line 1 'She ventured out at last'. Her boat, though a small one, would have had her living quarters under a wooden shelter or matting awning.

Verse 5, lines 1–2 'every note expressed a thought telling its tale of longing unfulfilled her whole life through'. Compare with *The Times* of 26 April 1965 reporting on the piano-playing of Vladimir Ashkenazy, '. . . it was as if he were communing with himself and we were privileged to hear his inmost thoughts'.

Verse 6, line 2 'Rainbow Skirt' and 'Lu Yao' were the names of two well-known songs, the first of a slow and the second of a quick measure.

Verse 11, line 2 'beauties like Ch'iu Niang'. A T'ang Dynasty Governor Li Tê-yü had a famous concubine called Hsieh Ch'iu-niang (which might be translated Autumn Beauty Hsieh). The name Ch'iu-niang accordingly became much used.

Verse 11, line 3 'The capital's gallants'. The Chinese refers to the 'youths of Wu-ling', which was one of the suburbs of the capital Ch'ang-an.

Verse 18, line 1 These three scenes are picked out as the best of the year – the river in spring, the Birthday of Flowers (a festival celebrating the opening of blossom in spring), and the autumn moon at night.

Ch'ang Hên Ko: 'The Song of Endless Sorrow', p. 219

Po Chü-i's poem is prefaced by a background note, written
not by the poet himself – as for 'The Song of a Guitar' – but by
a friend, Ch'ên Hung. But we have given here our own version
of the story.

The T'ang Emperor Hsüan-tsung at the age of about sixty-one
(A.D. 745) became infatuated by Yang Kuei-fei, the consort of
one of his sons, and duly appropriated her. He fell completely
under her spell, neglected his palace duties and promoted her
relatives to positions of power. One of his generals – of 'bar-
barian' descent – An Lu-shan, who had been made much of at
the Palace and was reputed to have been one of Yang Kuei-fei's
lovers, revolted in A.D. 755, first capturing Loyang and then
taking the capital, Ch'ang-an. The Emperor retreated to the
province of Szech'uan in the south-west, but not far from the
capital his army refused to move further unless his consort
Yang Kuei-fei and her brother were put to death. To save the
dynasty the Emperor was forced to agree, but such was his
distress that he abdicated then and there in favour of one of his
sons. Legend has it that Yang Kuei-fei was allowed to hang
herself from a tree. The revolutionaries in Ch'ang-an themselves
ran into trouble and An Lu-shan was killed by his own son.
Some eight years later the ex-Emperor was eventually able to
return to Ch'ang-an, leaving the son to whom he had abdicated
the title to rule. Back again, and still obsessed by the loss of his
consort, he fell under the influence of a Taoist priest who claimed
to be able to put him in touch with Yang Kuei-fei's spirit.

Verse 1, line 1 'Beauty that wrecks a kingdom'. This allusion
to a 'devastatingly beautiful woman', much used by poets, is
to a concubine who was introduced to the Emperor Wu of the
Han Dynasty as a beauty from whom 'one glance would over-
throw a city, and two a kingdom'.

Verse 1, line 4 'deep in the women's quarters'. See Note on
Poem No. 12, verse 2, line 2, p. 239.

Verse 2, line 4 'Six Palaces'. There were at one time six palace
buildings housing the womenfolk of the Emperor's entourage.
Later the expression 'Six Palaces' (Liu Kung) came simply
to mean 'The Palace Women's Apartments'.

Verse 3, line 1 The Hua-ch'ing Palace was built round the warm
springs feeding the Hua-ch'ing pool on Li-shan, the hill about
twenty miles east of the capital, Ch'ang-an. The story is told

that the Emperor had arranged to watch Yang Kuei-fei bathing from a secret vantage-point. (See also Verse 7, line 1, 'The Li Palace', i.e., the Hua-ch'ing Palace.)

Verse 4, line 2 'Hibiscus-dyed bed curtains'. The two characters 'fu jung' can be applied either to hibiscus, or to the lotus. The former was used as a dye, and being a short-lived, almost ephemeral, bloom, exemplified the pleasures of life; the lotus, which is the less orthodox translation, was used in the expression 'ping ti lien hua', meaning 'two lotus blossoms on one stalk' and was a symbol of 'mating' or union, and could in this context have been embroidered on the bed-curtains.

Verse 4, line 4 'The Emperor's early morning audience'. It was customary for the first court to be held at dawn.

Verse 7, line 5 'out of Yü-yang'. An Lu-shan, in command of the Imperial troops in the north-east, started his revolt from Yü-yang.

Verse 8, line 6 '. . . to placate the soldiers moth-browed beauty must die'. Yang Kuei-fei's and her brother's lives were demanded before the troops would proceed south. The first two characters of this line (wan chuan) can be variously translated. They could mean that the Emperor 'accommodated himself' (to the demands of his army) or that Yang Kuei-fei was 'submissive' or 'obedient' to them. A third possible meaning of these words is that she was 'strangled'.

In this context the Chinese 'horses' simply means 'the army' or 'the soldiers', as translated here.

Verse 12, line 3 'the Ma-wei slope' – the site of Yang Kuei-fei's death. It was said that the Emperor had the ground dug to recover her body, but without success.

Verse 13, line 2 'T'ai-yeh' was the name of a pool in the imperial palace grounds, and 'Wei-yang' one of the palaces. (See poem by Wang Ch'ing Hui, Poem No. 57, line 1, p. 185.)

Verse 14, line 1 'West Palace'. As the Emperor had abdicated in favour of one of his sons, he did not occupy the main palace (the Ta-ming-Kung) but a subsidiary one, the 'West Palace'.

Verse 14, line 3 'The actors of the Pear Garden'. It was this Emperor, Hsüan-tsung, who set up a special College of Dramatic Art to train actors and musicians. The college was originally sited in a pear garden and the name thereafter came to be, and still is, associated with the profession as 'The Folk/Brethren of the Pear Garden'.

Verse 14, line 4 'the eunuchs of the Pepper Room'. This name is supposed to have been given to a room in the Empress's quarters decorated with paintings of pepper trees, or covered with paper or plaster impregnated with pepper or pepper flower.

Verse 16, line 1 'Tiles of mandarin drake and duck'. These duck symbolized a happy marriage, and this name was applied therefore to interlocking tiles.

Verse 16, line 2 'Kingfisher cock-and-hen quilt'. As in the preceding line a pair of birds, probably embroidered on the quilt, are used as a contrast with the Emperor's loneliness. Schafer in 'The Vermilion Bird' – University of California Press, 1967, p. 238 – identifies this bird as the White-breasted King-fisher (Halcyon smyrnensis).

Verse 17, line 1 'A Tao-ist priest from Lin-Ch'iung' could either have been in the 'archivists' office' (hung-tu) or simply visiting the capital, 'Hung-tu' being the name of one of the gates of Ch'ang-an; we have chosen the second interpretation.

Verse 18, line 3 'The Yellow Springs'. The Tao-ist Hades.

Verse 19, line 3 'the Five Clouds' were the five-coloured clouds of green, white, red, black and yellow giving omens of plague, mourning, warfare and destruction, floods, and abundance, respectively.

Verse 19, line 5 'T'ai-chên'. This was a Tao-ist name signifying 'Elemental Truth' or 'Pure Gold' and was incidentally one of the names of endearment applied to Yang Kuei-fei. In this context the searcher does not know this and only refers to it as a Tao-ist immortal's name.

Verse 20, line 1 'At the western court'; the 'hsi hsiang' were the rooms on the west side of a courtyard. The lay-out of a Chinese palace, or indeed of a house of any size, demanded that the entrance lay to the south and one ascended as if in a vertical plane as one penetrated into the interior of the building. At or towards the northern end, through the various gates between one courtyard and the next, was the upper room (shang fang) which was the main room; to the side were the women's apart-ments, though they could also be behind (north of) the main rooms.

Verse 20, line 2 Hsiao-yü and Shuang-ch'eng – like T'ai-chên (see verse 19) – were Tao-ist names of immortals but again, as with T'ai-chên, the poet uses terms of endearment which had also been applied to Yang Kuei-fei's maid (Hsiao-yü) and to Yang Kuei-fei herself (Shuang-ch'eng).

Verse 23, line 3 'Chao-yang Palace' – at the capital in Ch'ang-an.

Verse 26, line 3 'The seventh day of the seventh month'. Note

261

that this is the day assigned by legend to the yearly reunion of the Weaver-girl and the Herd-boy – see Ch'in Kuan Note on Poem No. 26, p. 91.

Pattern and Rhyme

There are no divisions into separate verses in the Chinese original, which therefore reads without a break. Chinese commentators however have traditionally made divisions – after lines 8, 26, 32, 42, 56, 74, 88 and 100. Furthermore there is a majority of four-line sequences which rhyme on the first, second and fourth lines but not usually with the adjacent set of four lines. We have decided therefore to break up the poem into verses of four and six lines where it seemed appropriate, leaving a somewhat wider gap to show where the traditional divisions were made.

APPENDIX II

Tune-Titles and their Patterns

Poem number	Poet	P'u (Tune-title)	Pattern (Characters in each line)
1	Wei Ying Wu	Tiao Hsiao (Ling)	2 – 2 – 6 – 6 – 6 – 2 – 2 – 6
2	Chang Chih Ho	Yü Fu (Yü Ko Tzu)	7 – 7 – 3 – 3 – 7
3	Po Chü I	Lang T'ao Sha	7 – 7 – 7 – 7 Note: Not the same pattern used by Li Yü (Nan T'ang Hou Chu)
4	Wei Chuang	P'u Sa Man	7 – 7 – 5 – 5; 5 – 5 – 5 – 5
5	Anon	,,	See Poem 4
6	Fêng Yen Ssu	Yeh Chin Men	3 – 6 – 7 – 5; 6 – 6 – 7 – 5
7	,,	Tsui Hua Chien	7 – 5 – 5 – 5; 5 – 5 – 5 – 7 – 3 – 3
8	,,	Ch'iao T'a Chih (Tieh Lien Hua)	7 – 4 – 5 – 7 – 7; 7 – 4 – 5 – 7 – 7
9	P'an Lang	Chiu Ch'üan Tzu	4 – 7 – 7 – 5; 7 – 7 – 7 – 5
10	Lin Pu	Ch'ang Hsiang Ssu	3 – 3 – 7 – 5; 3 – 3 – 7 – 5
11	Chang Hsien	Kêng Lou Tzu	3 – 3 – 6 – 3 – 3 – 5; 3 – 3 – 6 – 3 – 3 – 5
12	,,	Ch'ing Mên Yin	5 – 6 – 7 – 4 – 5; 7 – 5 – 6 – 7
13	Yen Shu	Shan T'ing Liu	4 – 5 – 3 – 3 – 6 – 6 – 4; 7 – 7 – 3 – 6 – 6 – 6 – 4
14	Ou Yang Hsiu	Juan Lang Kuei	7 – 5 – 7 – 5; 3 – 3 – 5 – 7 – 5
15	Su Shih	Shao Nien Yu	4 – 4 – 5 – 4 – 4 – 5; 7 – 5 – 7 – 3 – 3
16	,,	Jui Chê Ku	7 – 7 – 7; 7 – 7 – 7 – 7
17	,,	Ch'in Yüan Ch'un	4 – 4 – 4 – 5 – 4 – 4 – 4 – 4 – 7 – 3 – 5 – 4; 2 – 4 – 3 – 5 – 4 – 4 – 4 – 7 – 3 – 5 – 4

Poem number	Poet	P'u (Tune-title)	Pattern (Characters in each line)
18	Su Shih	Chiang Ch'êng Tzu	7 – 3 – 3 – 4 – 5 – 7 – 3 – 3 ; 7 – 3 – 3 – 4 – 5 – 7 – 3 – 3
19	,,	Wan Ch'i Sha	7 – 3 – 3 – 4 – 5 – 7 – 3 – 3 ; 7 – 3 – 3 – 4 – 5 – 7 – 3 – 3
20	,,	,,	7 – 7 – 7 ; 7 – 7 – 7
21	,,	Ting Feng P'o	See Poem No. 20
22	,,	Wan Ch'i Sha	7 – 7 – 7 – 2 – 7 ; 7 – 2 – 7 – 7 – 2 – 7
23	,,	Lin Chiang Hsien	See Poem 20
24	,,		7 – 6 – 7 – 5 – 5 ; 7 – 6 – 7 – 5 – 5 Note: This differs slightly from the pattern used for Poem 60
25	Su Shih	Tieh Lien Hua (Ch'iao T'a Chih)	See Poem 8
26	Ch'in Kuan	Ch'üeh Ch'iao Hsien	4 – 4 – 6 – 7 – 7 ; 4 – 4 – 6 – 7 – 7
27	,,	Wang Hai Ch'ao	4 – 4 – 6 – 4 – 4 – 6 – 5 – 5 – 4 – 4 – 7 ; 6 – 5 – 4 – 4 – 4 – 6 – 5 – 5 – 4 – 4 – 7
28	Ho Chu	Shêng Ch'a Tzu	5 – 5 – 5 – 5 ; 5 – 5 – 5 – 5
29	Li Chih I	Pu Suan Tzu	5 – 5 – 7 – 5 ; 5 – 5 – 7 – 5
30	Chou Pang Yen	Shih Liu Tzu Ling	1 – 7 – 3 – 5
31	Ts'ai Shên	,,	See Poem 30
32	Ch'ên Chien Lung	,,	See Poem 30
33	Yüeh Fei	Man Chiang Hung	4 – 3 – 4 – 3 – 4 – 4 – 7 – 7 – 3 – 5 – 3 ; 3 – 3 – 3 – 3 – 5 – 4 – 7 – 7 – 3 – 5 – 3
34	Chu Tun Ju	Hao Shih Chin	See also calligraphy on p. 246 and translation included in Notes on Poems, p. 247 5 – 6 – 6 – 5 ; 7 – 5 – 5 – 6 – 5

Poem number	Poet	P'u (Tune-title)	Pattern (Characters in each line)
35	K'ang Yü Chih	Ts'ai Sang Tzu (Ch'ou Nu Erh Ling)	7 – 4 – 4 – 7; 7 – 4 – 4 – 4 – 7
36	Fan Ch'êng Ta	I Ch'in O	3 – 7 – 3 – 4 – 4; 7 – 7 – 3 – 4 – 4
37	Lu Yü	Pu Suan Tzu	See Poem No. 29
38	Hsin Ch'i Chi	Su Chung Ch'ing	7 – 5 – 6 – 5; 3 – 3 – 3 – 4 – 4 – 4
39	„	Shêng Ch'a Tzu	See Poem 28
40	„	„	See Poem 28
41	„	P'u Sa Man	See Poem 4
42	„	Ch'ing P'ing Lê	4 – 5 – 7 – 6; 6 – 6 – 6 – 6
43	„	„	See Poem 42
44	„	Hsi Chiang Yüeh	6 – 6 – 7 – 6; 6 – 6 – 7 – 6
45	„	„	See Poem 44
46	Hsin Ch'i Chi	Lang T'ao Sha	5 – 4 – 7 – 7 – 4; 5 – 4 – 7 – 7 – 4 Note: A different version from that used in Poem 3
47	„	Chê Ku T'ien	7 – 7 – 7 – 7; 3 – 3 – 7 – 7 – 7
48	„	P'o Chên Tzu	6 – 6 – 7 – 7 – 5; 6 – 6 – 7 – 7 – 5
49	„	Mu Lan Hua Man	5 – 3 – 3 – 5 – 4 – 6 – 8 – 6 – 6; 7 – 5 – 5 – 4 – 4 – 6 – 8 – 6 – 6
50	„	Shui Lung Yin	6 – 7 – 4 – 4 – 4 – 4 – 4 – 5 – 4 – 3 – 3; 6 – 3 – 4 – 4 – 4 – 4 – 4 – 4 – 3 – 6 – 4
51	Chiang K'uei	Hsing Hua T'ien Ying	7 – 7 – 7 – 2 – 6; 7 – 7 – 7 – 2 – 6
52	„	Tsui Yin Shang	5 – 6 – 4 – 5 – 6 – 4
53	„	Yü Mei Ling	4 – 5 – 3 – 4 – 5 – 5 – 4 – 4; 4 – 4 – 4 – 3 – 4 – 5 – 4 – 5 – 3 – 4

Poem number	Poet	P'u (Tune-title)	Pattern (Characters in each line)
54	Chiang K'uei	Ch'ang T'ing Yüan Man	3 – 4 – 4 – 4 – 4 – 3 – 4 – 3 – 3 – 5 – 3 – 4; 2 – 5 – 6 – 4 – 3 – 4 – 3 – 4 – 5 – 6
	,,	An Hsiang	4 – 5 – 4 – 4 – 7 – 6 – 3 – 4 – 3 – 4 – 5; 2 – 3 – 5 – 4 – 4 – 7 – 6 – 3 – 4 – 3 – 3 – 4 For tune and translation see Notes on Poems, pp. 254–5
55	Shih Ta Tsu	Shuang Shuang Yen	4 – 5 – 4 – 4 – 6 – 6 – 3 – 4 – 6 – 6; 2 – 4 – 5 – 4 – 4 – 6 – 6 – 3 – 4 – 6 – 6
56	Liu K'o Chuang	Yü Lou Ch'un	7 – 7 – 7 – 7; 7 – 7 – 7 – 7
57	Wang Ch'ing Hui	Man Chiang Hung	See Poem No. 33
58	Chiang Chieh	Yü Mei Jen	7 – 5 – 7 – 9; 7 – 5 – 7 – 9
59	Na-Lan Hsing-tê	Ju Mêng Ling	6 – 6 – 5 – 6 – 2 – 2 – 6
60	Ch'êng Hsi	Lin Chiang Hsien	7 – 6 – 7 – 4 – 5; 7 – 6 – 7 – 4 – 5 Pattern based on that used by Li Yü (Nan T'ang Hou Chu)

Notes: 1. A semi-colon denotes the end of a stanza.

2. Underlining of two numbers denotes that they have been represented in different anthologies as forming either one or two lines (i.e. 5 – 4 indicates that these nine characters form one line in some versions and two lines – of five and four characters respectively – in others).

APPENDIX III

Pronunciation of Chinese Names occurring in the Poems

Unless otherwise stated, in English 'a' is pronounced as in 'father', 'i' as in 'chin', 'ow' as in 'how', 'u' as in the French 'u'

Poem	Chinese name	Pronounced in English
1	Yen-chih-shan	Yen Jer Shan
2	Hsi-sai-shan	She Sai Shan ('ai' as 'eye')
	Cha-hsi	Ja She
	Sung	Soong
	Ch'ing-ts'ao	Ching Tsow
	Pa-ling	Ba Ling
3	Ch'ing-ts'ao	Ching Tsow
4	Chiang-nan	Ji-ang Nan
	Loyang	Lor Yang
	Wei	Way ('ay' as in 'day')
7	Chin-ling	Jin Ling
8	Ch'ing-ming	Ching Ming
10	Wu	Woo
	Yüeh	U-ay ('ay' as in 'day')
12	Ch'ing-ming	Ching Ming
13	Ch'in	Chin
	Nien-nu	Ni-en Noo
	Shu	Shoo
	Yang Ch'un	Yang Choon
15	Yü-hang	U Hang
	Ch'ang-O	Chang Er
17	Lu	Loo
	Yao	Yow
	Shun	Shoon

267

Poem	Chinese Name	Pronounced in English
24	Tung-p'o	Doong Por
33	Wan-Sui-Shan	Wan Sooay Shan ('ay' as in 'day')
	P'eng-hu-tien	Pung Hoo Di-en ('ung' as in 'hung')
	Han-yang	Han Yang
34	Tung-t'ing	Doong Ting
	Chien-t'ang	Chi-en Tang
	Tzu-ling	Tzer Ling
35	Feng I	Fung Ee ('ung' as in 'hung')
38	Liang-chou	Liang Joe
	T'ien-shan	Ti-en Shan
	Ts'ang-chou	Tsang Joe
40	Yü	U
41	Yü-Ku-t'ai	U Goo Tai ('ai' as 'eye')
	Ch'ang-an	Chang An
43	Chiang-nan	Ji-ang Nan
46	Ch'in	Chin
	Han	Han
48	Liu Pei	Li-oo Bay ('ay' as in 'day')
49	Ch'ang-O	Chang Er
50	Yüan Lung	Yuan Loong
51	Chin-ling	Jin Ling
54	Wei	Way ('ay' as in 'day')
	Ping	Bing
57	T'ai-yeh	Tai I-eh ('ai' as 'eye')
	Ch'ang-O	Chang Er
'The Song	Hsün-yang	Shun Yang
of a	Lu Yao	Loo Yow
Guitar'	Hsia-mo	Shi-a Mor
	Ch'iu Niang	Chi-oo Ni-ang
	Fou-liang	Foe Li-ang
	P'en-p'u	Pun Poo ('un' as in 'bun')
	Chiang-chou	Ji-ang Joe
The Song	Yang	Yang
of Endless	Hua-ch'ing	Hwa Ching
Sorrow	Li	Lee
	Yü-yang	U Yang
	Chien-ko	Ji-en Ger
	O-mei Shan	Er May Shan ('ay' as in 'day')

Poem	Chinese name	Pronounced in English
The Song	Szechwan	Ser Choo-an
of Endless	Ma-wei	Ma Way ('ay' as in 'day')
Sorrow	T'ai-yeh	Tai I-eh ('ai' as 'eye')
	Wei-yang	Way Yang ('ay' as in 'day')
	Wu-t'ung	Woo Toong
	Lin-ch'iung	Lin Chi-oong
	T'ai-chen	Tai Jun ('ai' as 'eye'; 'un' as in 'bun')
	Hsiao-yü	Shi-ow U
	Shuang-Ch'eng	Shoo-ang Chung ('ung' as in 'hung')
	Chao-Yang	Jow Yang
	Ch'ang-an	Chang An
	Ch'ang-sheng	Chang Shung ('ung' as in 'hung')

INDEX

271